NEWNEW ZEALAND HOUSES

NEW NEW ZEALAND HOUSES

PATRICK REYNOLDS AND JOHN WALSH

GODWIT

advanced simplicity

Patrick Reynolds is grateful for the support of Canon in this project.

A catalogue record for this book is available from the National Library of New Zealand

A GODWIT BOOK
published by
Random House New Zealand
18 Poland Road, Glenfield, Auckland, New Zealand
www.randomhouse.co.nz

Random House International
Random House
20 Vauxhall Bridge Road
London, SW1V 2SA
United Kingdom

Random House Australia (Pty) Ltd
20 Alfred Street, Milsons Point, Sydney
New South Wales 2061, Australia

Random House South Africa Pty Ltd
Isle of Houghton
Corner Boundary Road and Carse O'Gowrie
Houghton 2198, South Africa

Random House Publishers India Private Ltd
301 World Trade Tower, Hotel Intercontinental Grand Complex
Barakhamba Lane, New Delhi 110 001, India

First published 2007

© 2007 text John Walsh; photographs Patrick Reynolds, except Hall House, Paroa Bay House and Walker
House © ACP Magazines, reproduced by kind permission; cartoon page 15 © Malcolm Walker.

The moral rights of the authors have been asserted

ISBN 978 1 86962 129 2

Design: Nick Turzynski, redinc.
Cover photographs: Patrick Reynolds
Cover design: redinc.
Printed in China by Everbest Printing Co Ltd

CONTENTS

To my parents, I.B. and M.L., who unwittingly started me on this. PR

To Catherine Hammond and Xavier and Nicholas. JW

ACKNOWLEDGEMENTS

Our thanks to the architects for their enthusiasm and assistance and especially to their clients, who put up with Patrick crawling all over their houses and kindly allowed us to publish them here. Our thanks also to the team at Random House for their labours, to Sjoerd Langeveld of Labtec for prepress work, and to Malcolm Walker for his cartoon.

THIS HAS BEEN A very good century for New Zealand architects so far. In fact, never have so many of them had it so good. A sustained period of prosperity has meant more construction, and therefore more architects and more and bigger practices. Busy architectural firms, particularly in Auckland and Wellington, have found it hard to keep up. That most attractive professional prospect, the graduate with several years' experience — a person both young *and* useful — has never been more eligible. Another sign that the profession's human resources have been stretched has been the presence in metropolitan architecture offices of architects from all over — from the UK, Ireland, France, Germany, North and South America . . . New Zealand, traditionally an exporter of architectural talent, probably hasn't had such an international architectural scene since the country accepted, rather warily, a group of Middle European émigré architects in the 1930s.

It's true that, as any architect in any practice in the country will tell you, not all busyness is productive. The proportion of an architect's day spent dealing with the paper piles extruded by legislators and bureaucrats grows larger every year. (As Malcolm Walker suggested in one of his regular cartoons for *Architecture New Zealand*, the object of such relentless documentary production seems to be the provision of ample legal cover for every official posterior.) Nevertheless, to older architects who experienced the thin years of the 1990s, the fat years of this decade must seem rather miraculous. (If there's wood around, now might be a good time to touch it.) Architects who regret the imposition of onerous compliance regimes should perhaps reflect on the importance to their profession, and their wallets, of a government which, during its successive terms of office, has been committed to infrastructural catch-up. They might concede, too, that the bureaucratic chastisement of the construction industry was hardly unprovoked; one might say that Dad's taken back the keys of the car after too many incidents of careless driving.

It might seem crass to begin this discussion with talk of money, but that's where architecture starts. No money, no architecture, or rather, and more properly, no Architecture — big A architecture being the work of big A architects, designers who have earned the right to an upper-case appellation by passing university courses and then taking the time and making the effort to get through the profession's own examinations. All the Architecture in this book is by Architects (having established the conventions, we can now drop the capitals). The assumption is not so much that only the work of registered architects really registers, but that qualifications are a pretty reliable guide to competence. In do-it-yourself New Zealand this might seem a heretical position, but in architecture, it holds true. Not all architects have the talent or opportunity to design good buildings, but in general, good buildings are designed by architects. Want a negative proof? Drive north of Auckland and look at the new tracts of developer-driven suburbia.

Back to money: a nation would have to be in a pretty dire state to fail to produce any architecture. (Like many other countries, New Zealand during the early years of the Depression came close.) Even — especially — when times are tough, certain types of buildings, schools and hospitals, for example, courts and prisons, must be built, and must be designed by architects. But other buildings are, if not a luxury, then at least optional. No building is more discretionary than the architect-designed house, historically the forté of New Zealand architecture. Why should this be so?

This is a small and suburban nation, built, in its modern settler form, from scratch in less than 200 years. It is a country in which home ownership has been a political priority, a culturally defining characteristic and, certainly for much of the twentieth century, a realisable aspiration. And, on the other hand, there haven't been a lot of big buildings to go around. It's only relatively recently that architects have been able to focus on the larger scale. Even now, the development of any building over 15 storeys is likely

INTRODUCTION

to be a unique event in any year in any New Zealand city outside Auckland. The necessary condition for bespoke residential architecture is a reasonable amount of affluence; there has been more money around for residential architecture in the last decade than, probably, ever before. The only precedent, perhaps, was that short and what now seems inglorious period in the mid-1980s, when sudden economic deregulation stimulated latent appetites for many of life's finer things, including architect-designed houses.

Enough about means; more edifyingly, let's consider motives. (Money might be necessary for architecture, but it's certainly not a sufficient reason for good residential architecture.) An architect-designed house must be one of life's richest treats. Fancy having a house with spaces designed to fit and enhance your life! The norm, of course, is making do with hand-me-down spaces expressive of the demographic realities and domestic ideologies of a dead generation, or coming to terms with spaces organised to maximise a developer's return. It's not really until you walk through or just sit down in some well-designed houses — houses shaped around particular, not generic lives — that you realise how spatially awkward many of our dwellings are. They're not resolved; in many cases, they're neurotic. (Well, they're suburban — what should one expect?)

It's not necessarily cheapness that's the cause of clumsiness. Many big, new, expensive houses don't conceal designer incompetence, they magnify it. Given the qualitative difference that good architecture brings, and considering there often isn't much financial difference between the work of able architects and mediocre work done to boilerplate designs, it seems surprising that more people don't engage the services of a serious spatial professional. Yes, architects *are* professionals and, therefore, in a country where lower-middle-class resentments run deep and DIY competence has been the mark of a Kiwi bloke, perhaps prima facie suspect. But, come on, architects are not lawyers — at least, provided the builder has got his sums right and materials suppliers are only moderately greedy, you'll have something to show for all those billed hours. Wellington architect Chris Kelly (two of whose projects feature in this book) also wonders about a national character trait that seems rather self-defeating. People 'don't challenge their process when it comes to spending money on a building,' Kelly says. 'Why, if you're going to spend even 150 grand on a bach, wouldn't you spend a portion of that taking some good advice?' The answer, Kelly suspects, is that New Zealanders 'still operate in a property culture, not a design culture.' (*Houses NZ*, 3, 2007.)

SO WHO HAVE ARCHITECTS been designing houses for in this fortunate era of the profession? Well, for a start, themselves, as evidenced by several of the houses in this book: Kelly's Oriental Bay House and Dave Launder's Kaitawa Road House, and the holiday houses on the Kapiti and Coromandel coasts by Gerald Parsonson and Ken Crosson. It is every architect's dream to design his or her own home. (It might be every architect spouse's nightmare: notoriously, architect's houses are never quite finished.) Houses, since the heyday

Wakatipu Basin House,
Fearon Hay Architects
— pages 52–67.

of modernism, have served as architectural laboratories, an analogy which, unfortunately, suggests social engineering as much as programmatic experimentation. (What does it make the client? Guinea pig? Lab rat?) But who better to try all those ideas out on than oneself, and one's understanding family? Just about every architect who has designed his or her own house will declare it to have been an improving as well as an instructive experience. They now know, for example, the pain of running out of money.

Other, more lucrative, categories of house clients include people extending an existing house or replacing it with a contemporary design on the same site; people wanting to build on a piece of subdivided suburban land or a greenfield site; and people building a second — or maybe third — dwelling for use as a holiday house. Examples of all these project types are in this book. Without wishing to be tautological, architects design houses for those who can afford them.

At the end of the market where leading architects tend to operate, clients have to have accumulated some capital, and that is likely to mean that, unless they have been precociously successful in their careers or winners in life's genetic lottery, they may well be of a certain age. This is not, it should be stressed, universally true. Some of the projects in this book are houses designed and built to modest budgets for clients with determination and commitment (the Hughes-Kinugawa House and the Arapai-Urale House, for example). But, in the upper stratum of residential architecture, one does find the relatively young practice — men, one might say, of

mode — designing houses for clients who are formed people. They have 'baggage', one might say, or at least familiar and comfortable objects accumulated down the years.

What am I saying here? Perhaps just that both architects and clients have to be careful about communication. I remember visiting a house in Central Otago — not one of the houses in this book — and being impressed by the obvious rapport between the clients and their architect. One of the clients impressed upon me that the architect had really, really listened. The remark was repeated like an instruction delivered to an idiot (OK, OK, I hear you), but the message being implied almost as strongly as that being expressed was that some architects *don't* listen. It's not just a matter of following the letter of a brief; architects have to somehow intuit unspoken desires, interpret vague yearnings. (Sometimes, too, they have to contemplate clients' cutting files — reams of inspirational material from international design magazines.) Successful architects, like many professionals who provide personal services, are psychologically astute. They're practised in the arts of placation, reassurance and suggestion, and they have to be discreet; architects learn a lot of secrets in the course of designing a house and overseeing its construction.

SOMETIMES ONE DOES SENSE — is it a matter of detection, or perhaps just projection? — some incongruity about a very competently designed and assembled up-market house. In such a house, now and then, a whiff of bemusement seems to suggest some

Kaitawa House,
Dave Launder Architect
— pages 128–137.

cross-purpose communication. Are some new houses too young for the people who have commissioned them? Too lean and hard? We're crossing, here, into the territory of recent controversy. If any development has typified New Zealand's metropolitan, and subsequently influenced its provincial residential, architecture since 2000 it has been the hegemony of what might be described as neo-modernism, or minimalism as it is more commonly called. Minimalism, one might say, is a dialectical outcome of the successful struggle of postmodernism against modernism. Having abandoned its social agenda and drifted free of its philosophical underpinnings, modernism had long ago lost all vitality. By the 1970s — certainly by the 1980s — modernism was just hanging on; PoMo put it out of its misery. With its relativism and borrowings, its tricks and games and casuistries, postmodernism was a perfect style for its meretricious times; it's to architecture what spin-doctoring is to politics.

Local architects had some fun with postmodernism — and their efforts look pretty funny today — but all jokes run their course. The excesses of postmodernism invited reprisal. Modernism returned, or rather, its formal language did. One can see why: postmodernism is all adjectives; modernism is a plainer construct of nouns and verbs. Of course, the language of this restored modernism doesn't really signify much, which might explain its attractions. It's a suitable style for a certain sort of affluent residential architecture: it's legible and neutral, and it's a good backdrop for art. It's pretty safe. Default positions aren't necessarily

bad things; some imaginations we should be saved from. The International Style, for example, that great standby of mid-twentieth century architecture, served this country rather well. Look, for example, at Plischke and Firth's Massey House (1953) in Wellington and the Wanganui War Memorial Hall (1958) by Geoffrey Newman, Gordon Smith and Anthony Greenhough, and at late 1950s and early 1960s Auckland houses by Heinrich Kulka and Vladimir Cacala.

One doesn't have to be a *Wallpaper* subscriber to think that the problem with the International Style in New Zealand was that there wasn't more of it — if, that is, if it were to have been competently executed. And there's the rub with minimalism. Because it is a genre of architecture that prizes clarity it is unforgiving of solecism. The results of the clumsy aping of a ubiquitous style can be seen in the real estate supplements of the weekend newspapers. Besides being a depressing record of our cupidity and a confirmation that architecture as it is practised by many architects is merely, and despite their protestations, an adjunct of the real estate 'industry', even the small photographs in these supplements expose the shortcomings of a style that has become an orthodoxy. Minimalist architecture, to be really successful, depends upon maximalist expenditure. Programmatic coherence is just the start; minimalism is a very refined materialism. Finishes, surfaces, furnishings all matter.

Fearon Hay is, perhaps, the practice most closely associated with local minimalism. Their houses, as exemplified by their three projects in this book, are

Butler House,
Fearon Hay Architects
— pages 164–177.

cool and slick and glamorous. (The partners in the firm probably do not feel flattered by their various imitators, if they give them any thought.) Their houses, too, are often pavilion-like, or include pavilion elements. The pavilion is a perfect expression of modernism and a building type beloved, in any case, of architects everywhere: it approaches that architectural nirvana of the structure-less structure. The pavilion, too, has particular appeal in a country with such a pronounced, and understandable, proclivity for the view. If a view is there, we can't seem to get enough of it. (Can you have too much of a good thing? An interesting aspect of many of the houses in this book is the framing strategy adopted in picturesque places. Architects, it seems, quite enjoy a little burlesque entertainment.) For some critics, though, a pavilion's transparency suggests vacuity, an absence of an inner life. This seems a bit rough: people in glass houses, they should be stoned? The gist of the criticism of pavilion houses, and minimalist houses in general, is that they're not sufficiently homely. You know — comfortable, nurturing, cosy. They're so composed, it's hard to relax.

I'm not sure about this; I suspect clients' spatial expectations have just expanded with societal affluence. Maybe as we've filled out, so too have our houses. Another memory comes to mind, that of a visit to John Scott's Martin House (1970), near Hastings. The house is beautiful and clever, but now it seems as if was built on something less than a 1:1 scale. The children's bedrooms, for example, look like cells for a dwarf order of monks. Modern kids, with all their games and gear,

would think they were cupboards.

Although minimalism, a boxed package of the classic modernist materials (concrete, steel, wood), has been popular in the past decade, not every significant New Zealand architect has been a card-carrying member of the neo-mod squad. Architects are products of their times, of course, and cannot but be influenced by contemporary styles or approaches. Even Malcolm Walker, a fine but hardly a dandy architect, has admitted that 'You are driven by what the style of the day is . . . There's always a certain sort of fashion to what you do.' (*Houses NZ*, 4, 2007) But architects aren't just influenced just by what's in: their work is circumscribed by the circumstances of their times in other ways, too. They work with what they've got — the sites and budgets, tools and materials available to them.

And, of course, good architects contrive to transcend those circumstances. The work of David Mitchell and Julie Stout, for example, cannot usefully be placed under the rubric of neo-modernism, or anything else. Mitchell and Stout's residential architecture has evolved over a period of several decades now. In the domestic work of this practice one appreciates the ambivalent position of really good architects who, in a way, are providers of surplus aesthetic value. Squeezing in stuff is all just part of the job on every upmarket house, of course, but it's impossible not be unsettled by the thought of an architect such as David Mitchell — humane, artful, and very experienced — sitting down to figure out spaces for four-wheel-drive cars and big television sets. One can only

Vernon Retreat, Malcolm
Walker Architects
— pages 66–75.

applaud the subversive campaign against amenity being waged on Great Barrier Island by Herbst Architects.

Other houses in this book also buck the prevailing trend. Stevens Lawson, for example, seem to be running an experiment in organic design that, at the high end of residential architecture, must be unique. Malcolm Walker himself, son of the pluvial West Coast, never gave up on the gable. Chris Kelly and Architecture Workshop manage to marry reason and caprice. Dave Launder, in his house, has just followed his heart. There is still plenty of room for individual architectural expression in this country, as much scope, perhaps, as in the rumpty old 1970s, despite the steady accretion of rules and regulations. (One of the perennial mysteries of planning is how whole mediocre suburbs can be flagged through by local authorities while a highly competent, albeit somewhat singular design for an inner-city house can be subjected to years of inquisition and obstruction.)

SOMETHING ELSE THAT IS apparent, to gauge from the projects in this book, is that architects and clients find each other (even, that is, when architect and client are not the same person). That is, residential architecture is a relationship in which each side gets the partner they deserve. Some clients are prescriptive, others are more biddable; occasionally, it seems they've just been along for the ride. For their part, some architects are headstrong and some are more pliant. But in many cases, the relationship has been a close collaboration. It's a big deal to commission an architect-designed house, and it's quite an achievement for everyone to have remained friends during the intense process of design and construction.

Another thing that should be obvious is that architecture is not democratic in its occurrence or its practice. It can't happen to everyone, it won't take place on every street, it won't be common in many suburbs. The houses in this book indicate, not by design but also not by coincidence, those parts of the country where the best architectural practices are most active: Auckland, where almost half of the country's architectural practices are based; the Bay of Islands, the Coromandel Peninsula, Wellington and its Kapiti Coast and Wairarapa hinterlands, and Central Otago. This distributive pattern is tied to two contemporary phenomena: the development of the coasts, and the rise of a sophisticated holiday architecture.

For the practices whose work is represented in this book, New Zealand is one architectural market. It should be noted there are other able practices in New Zealand, and there are many other well-designed houses, but they couldn't be in this book, for one reason or other — the owners' resistance to publicity, the architects' disinclination to publish, the not-quite-finished state of the projects, the perhaps questionable judgment of writer and photographer. There is also a new stratum of architect-designed houses in New Zealand now, houses which are to all intents invisible to the rest of the populace, and maybe even hidden to history. This book, therefore, cannot and does not pretend to be a survey of all of the best contemporary residential architecture, right now. It does, though, present some of the best work of some of the best practices in what have been some of the best years for New Zealand architecture. And it presents some of the best work of New Zealand's best architectural photographer. Maybe it's about the canon; certainly it's about the Canon.

van Asch House,

Felicity Wallace architects

— pages 218–231.

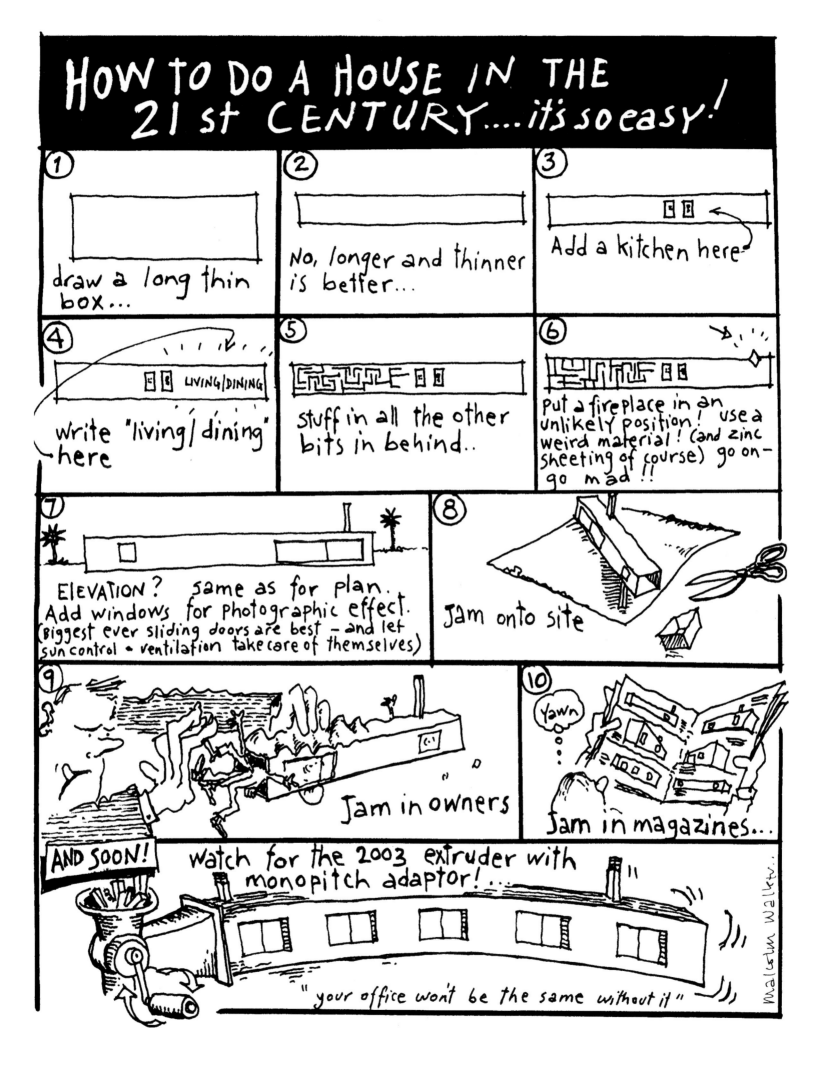

RIVERSIDEROADHOUSE

1

ARCHITECTURE
WORKSHOP

WAIRARAPA

2004

ON THIS PROJECT CLIENTS of
independent mind found an architect never
at a loss for singular ideas. Thirty years
ago Neil and Dawn McCallum made the
highly rational decision — Neil is a scientist — to
defy conventional wisdom and start a vineyard near
Martinborough. At the time, the small Wairarapa
town was off the map of the known wine world.
Now, it's in all the wine atlases and one reason for its
celebrity has been the performance of the McCallums'
Dry River winery.

The enterprise is a successful union of scientific
method and exacting standards of production (no
irrigation, hand leaf-picking, low cropping). Or, less
prosaically, Dry River wine is the expression of its
makers' desire to understand a particular site and
discover what it, uniquely, may yield.

The winemaker's approach to place is not so
different from the architect's (both could be described
as terroir-ists). In the case of this house, designed
for the McCallums by Chris Kelly of Architecture
Workshop, the similarities between the clients' and
the architect's way of doing things are particularly
evident. Among the commonalities are a commitment
to research, a willingness to pursue unorthodox
solutions, and the confidence to acknowledge and
examine antecedents. For both clients and architect,
reference is a matter of some reverence: Dry River
is a New World winery with an Old World respect
for craft; the Riverside Road House openly cites
distinguished precedents, among them, and most
clearly, Louis Kahn's Kimbell Art Museum in Fort
Worth, Texas (1972).

This is a surprising house, not just because of what
and where it is, although the concrete vault is hardly
a typical form in Wairarapa domestic architecture.
It is a romance, really, produced by reason — a
building that induces wonderment, generated by
clients and architect who are uncommonly analytical.
(Perhaps this is no paradox at all: imagination is
not incompatible with hard thinking, and brainy
discourse can still allow for the intangible qualities
of good wine, and good architecture.) The house is
also unexpectedly serene. High up above a plain, one
might expect a buffeting; encountering a house by an
architect so clearly in ideological surplus one might
anticipate some restlessness. Neither happens; the
house keeps its peace, just as the clients and their
architect held their nerve.

It could be said that clients and architect were
made for each other, if it weren't that suitability is only
retrospectively obvious. Once they had chosen their
site, the McCallums had several requirements for their
first architect-designed house, which followed from
some definite likes and dislikes. They wanted solidity
('We didn't want to feel the elements,' Neil McCallum
says); refuge ('a place that feels like a home'); and
permanence ('I hate the wastefulness of 50-year
houses'). The McCallums had lived in a simple, mass-
produced house for twenty years; they'd had it with
wood, and wanted a house with a concrete roof. They
wanted a house strong enough to stand up to a one-in-
650-years earthquake.

This may seem like a brief for a bunker (and the

house is dug into its hillside site), but the clients also sought other qualities, which they associated with Kelly's architecture: an integration of building with landscape, and a bringing-in of the outside. There was something else, too, which suggested the clients' wish to transcend architecture-as-prescription and their aversion to the recent vogue for the house-as-box: their relatively new-found admiration for the Moorish architecture of southern Spain. Curves and courtyards, stone and water, outlook and seclusion — in the Riverside Road House the tropes of Andalusia receive an antipodean treatment.

Architecture Workshop buildings characteristically counterpose heavy (solid) and light (ephemeral) elements. That material juxtaposition was incompatible with the brief and, perhaps, the site for this house. But the effect of the strategy, that is, the provision of shelter and the experience of space, has been realised. The vehicle is the barrel vault form that, repeated a dozen times, in single- or double-room iterations, envelopes the house.

Vaulting ambition, all right; the more one thinks about this house the more audacious it seems. The vault has some heavy connotations. It's the shape of silence — of churches, cellars and crypts. Kelly has taken a subterranean form and dragged it up to the top of a hill and opened it to the light. Much of the serenity of this house can be ascribed to the vaulted roofs and the rhythm of their repetition. With a flat top the house would feel totally different — meaner, lower, closer. Instead, maximum headroom: nothing like a 30-tonne concrete vault to take the weight off

one's mind. Circulation through the house is, logically, but with appropriate contrariness, across the grain of the vaults.

Two other elements of this house are crucial to its success: the courtyards sited to give various options for outdoor shelter, and the windows that frame views (but, deliberately, never whole views) extending to the South Island. The central or 'sky' courtyard, enclosed by walls faced with split Oamaru stone, lulled by a fountain, is at the heart of the plan. Cloistered, shaded and decorated only by its materials, this is a space that would appeal as much to a monk as a Moor and, like the vaulted interiors, one that is rarely experienced in this country's architecture.

There is a suggestion of renunciation, too, in the handling of the windows. Delayed gratification might be a better way of putting it; there's so much to see, especially on the south and west sides where the site drops steeply away, that it doesn't have to be seen all at once. Kelly has been careful to differentiate the views, and he convinced his clients to give them timber frames. (The clients now welcome a bit of wooden relief from concrete, stone and steel.) There's one framed view, in particular, that rewards Kelly's careful composition: a view to the west, down to and across the flats to the Ruamahanga River and then up to successively higher parallel ranges. In the afternoon light it resembles a backdrop as much as a prospect — generic quattrocento Umbrian countryside, stretching out behind a castle on the hill.

1   central courtyard
2   gallery
3   lake ferry courtyard
4   fire place
5   dining
6   living
7   ruamahanga courtyard
8   kitchen
9   family
10   morning courtyard
11   bed
12   bath
13   study
14   mudroom
15   cellar
16   garage
17   machine room
18   store
19   services area

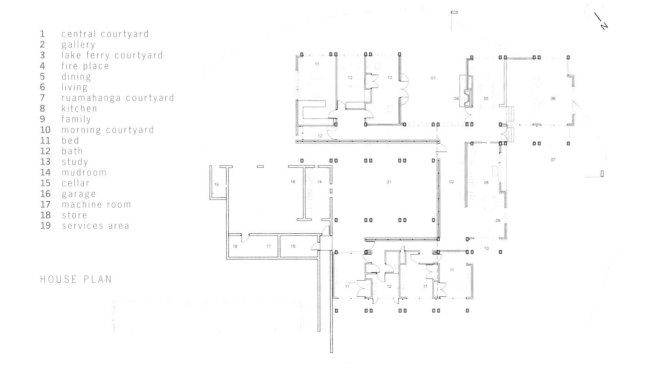

HOUSE PLAN

Above: Looking west through the house from the Lake Ferry courtyard.

Right: The central courtyard, with its water feature.

Facing page: Repeated forms of the pre-cast concrete vaults.

Above: Bedrooms opening
onto the courtyard at the
north-east.

Facing page: Looking west
over the vaulted roof forms
to the Ruamahunga River and
Tararua Ranges.

View from the gallery, to the
main courtyard, with the Lake
Ferry courtyard on the left.

Above: Looking through the
kitchen to the dining room.

Above right: View of the
gallery from the main entry,
looking towards the
bedroom wing.

Looking west over the house, which is dug into the side of a Wairarapa hill.

ARAPAI–URALE HOUSE

2

MALCOLM WALKER
ARCHITECTS

FREEMANS BAY,
AUCKLAND

2004

Previous spread: The Arapai–
Urale family in the hall of their
Freemans Bay house.

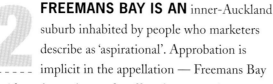

2 **FREEMANS BAY IS AN** inner-Auckland suburb inhabited by people who marketers describe as 'aspirational'. Approbation is implicit in the appellation — Freemans Bay residents have plenty of stuff, and, apparently, an appetite for ever more of it. It hasn't always been this way; for much of the suburb's 150-year history it was a working-class district. Even that might be putting it too grandly; for decades, if residents 'aspired' to be anything, it was to be proletarian.

Up until the 1970s, the standard unit of Freemans Bay housing stock was the worker's cottage of Victorian or Edwardian vintage and, normally, fatigued state. Gentrification got going a generation ago, but it took a while for Freemans Bay to become respectable. When Arnette Arapai was growing up in the suburb some neighbours kept chickens, others had pigs in the back yard, and 'there were streets we were told not to go down'. Architecture, as recently as twenty or thirty years ago, was something that mostly happened on the other side of town.

Freemans Bay, like Ponsonby up the ridge and Grey Lynn down the other side, was one of the early sites of mid-twentieth century settlement for Pacific Island migrants to Auckland. Many of the Pacific Island families who made their homes in these suburbs have left the area, but not the Arapais. Arnette's mother, a New Zealand-born Nuiean, and her father, who is from the Cook Islands, bought a house in Freemans Bay in 1976 and have stayed through the changes in the demographic tides. Compared to the forlorn condition of much of New Zealand suburbia, Freemans Bay is a

diverting place, close to the centre of the city but still human in scale. Arnette Arapai is loyal to the locale, although it's less communal than it once was (she and her husband, Tati Urale, seem to have taken the paucity of children in the neighbourhood as a personal challenge). She gets a kick, too, from confounding the not uncommon well-I-never reaction to her living situation: 'A Pacific Island family . . . living in an architect-designed house in Freemans Bay!'.

When Arnette, with Tati Urale, discussed this house with Malcolm Walker — 'a friend of a friend' — she told the architect 'All I want is a pantry and a shower.' Oh, and a few other things: a balcony where Tati could smoke, an island in the kitchen, and — later — red paint on the front door. Apart from these few particular requirements what the clients wanted was a practical house; with kids to accommodate — there are six children now, ranging from toddler to teenager — and an extended family to host, the house could not be 'precious'. How the final form was arrived at was up to Malcolm Walker. 'You're the expert' are words an architect must hope to hear, and in response, Arnette says, 'Malcolm suggested a lot of things.'

The house formally alludes to the neighbouring cottages in this 'special character' zone, but the architect was far more concerned with now than then. Inside, 'a variety of loose spaces' have been designed with various activities in mind, 'from rugby in the hall to homework upstairs, from nursing infants to saxophone practice'. It's all on in this house, and often all at the same time. Life spills over; few activities are confined to specific rooms. There are screens and doors that could close off

GROUND FLOOR PLAN

1 entry
2 hall
3 bed
4 bathroom
5 retreat
6 family
7 kitchen
8 smoking deck

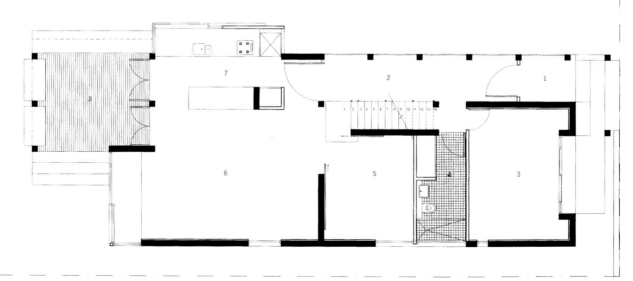

various areas but this is not a family inclined to jealously patrol personal space. Moreover, the house frequently is a base for visiting family and friends. 'We've had thirty people staying in the place,' Arnette says. To the clients, the new house seemed big: 'We weren't used to space,' Arnette says. 'We'd been living in a two-bedroom house . . . at first, the kids wouldn't sleep in their own rooms. They were in our room for months.'

The design for this house and its material composition express an architect's understanding of how a family actually lives; there's no sense of a designer telling clients how they ought to live. ('I'm not a stylist,' Malcolm Walker has said, 'and I'm not interested in building houses as objects.') The house, in the architect's words, is 'simple, flexible, comfortable and robust'. Materials are tough and durable: strapped and lined concrete block walls; floors of polished concrete and jarrah; over the living area, a perforated, acoustically lined zinc ceiling. The hall on the east side leading from the front door to the kitchen and living areas — a corridor that no doubt serves as a running track, wrestling rink and rugby pitch — is clad on one side in fibreglass roofing sheets, punctuated with push-out openings. Besides admitting light, the translucent cladding provides an almost delicate contrast to the house's predominantly solid construction.

The overtly communal spaces — living area, kitchen and balcony — are at the north end of the house. Behind the big living room, with its generous window seat — 'a Malcolm signature', Arnette says — there is a dining room that could serve as a 'retreat'. It's perhaps the one space that the clients, who specifically requested it, haven't quite figured out how to use, probably because in this family there is just no expectation of escape. There is no suggestion from the clients of anything other than complete satisfaction with their house. Arnette Arapai says she'll never sell it.

A long-time cartoonist, as well as an experienced architect, Malcolm Walker doesn't take himself too seriously. But he is serious about addressing the needs of his clients, one reason why his projects are successful and his professional relationships often become friendships. In a recent interview (*Houses New Zealand*, 4, 2007) Walker described the often intense process of designing a house for the people who are actually going to live in it as a privilege. 'It's easy to forget that . . . because you've done it so often and you'd probably go mad if you took it too personally. But you have to be aware that that's what's happening. You mustn't forget that.'

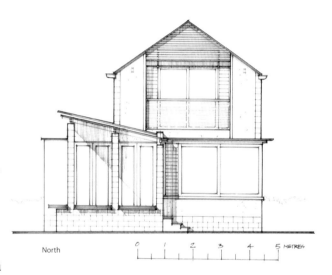

North

0 1 2 3 4 5 METRES

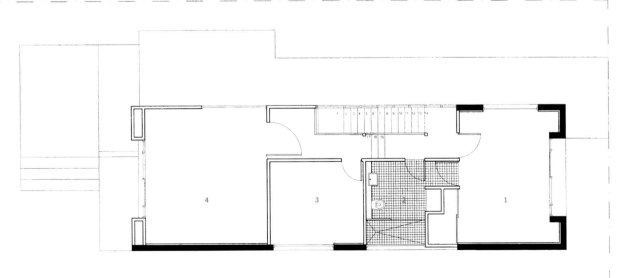

FIRST FLOOR PLAN

1 bedroom
2 bathroom
3 bedroom
4 kids' bedroom

Right: Smoking deck at the north-west of the house.

Below: The house from the street, showing openings for air circulation on the translucent north wall.

Facing page: Rear of the house, looking east towards the city centre.

Right: Looking through the house from the front door, along the light-filled hall on the north side.

Lower right: Looking from the kitchen back to the front door.

ARAPAI–URALEHOUSE

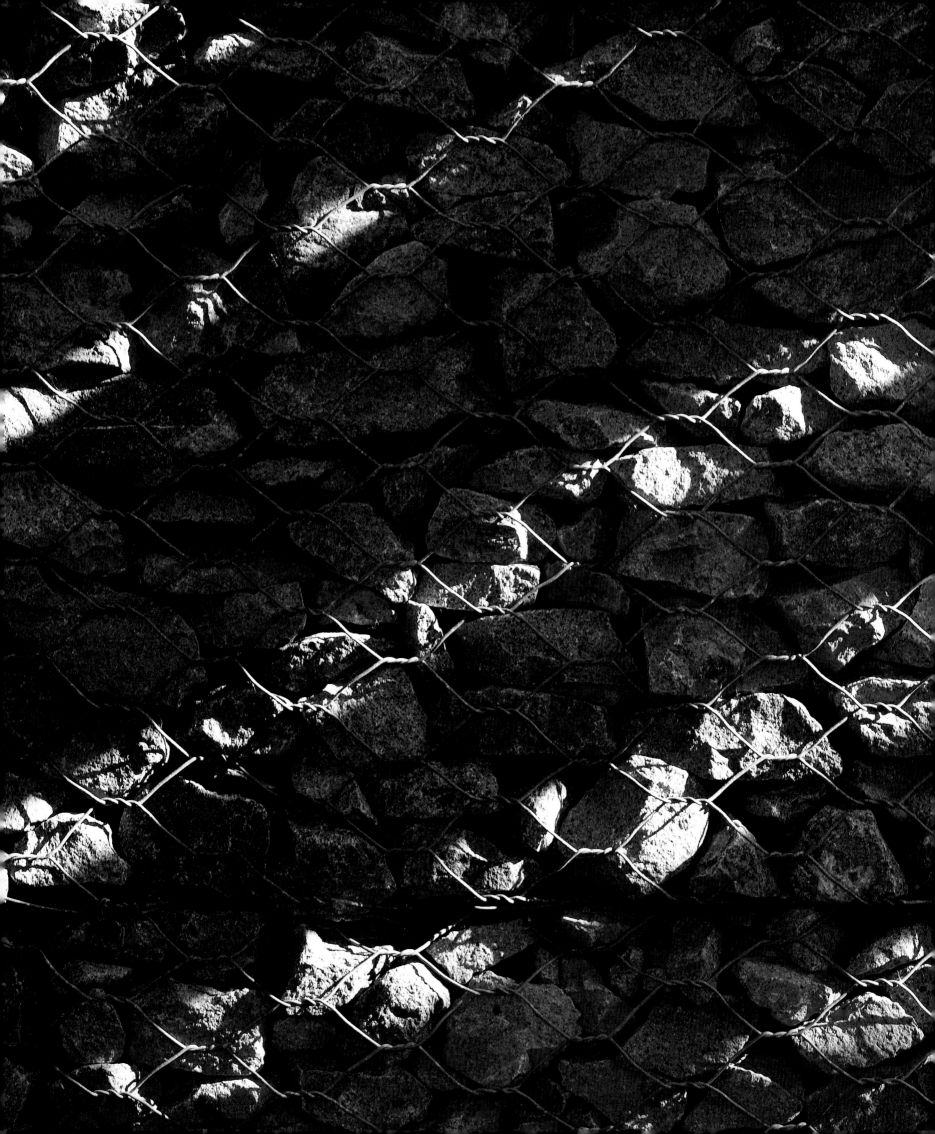

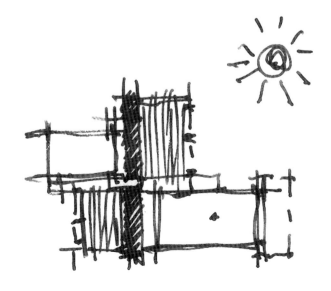

LINDALEBACH

3

HERBST
ARCHITECTS

GREAT BARRIER
ISLAND

2006

THE LINDALE BACH ON Great Barrier Island is the latest and most sophisticated in a series of beach houses designed by Lance and Nicky Herbst in the decade since they migrated from Cape Town to Auckland. Deceptively simple in its appearance, the bach, on closer inspection, is a complex building that exhibits the architects' attention to detail and their consuming interest in assemblage. It demonstrates, too, the progress of the architects' ongoing experiment with what New Zealanders would regard as *the* national material — timber — and *the* national type — the bach. And, not least, it expresses some rather definite ideas about the conduct of holiday life. The architects have a vision of the good life on Great Barrier Island, and it certainly isn't suburban.

Lightweight construction has typified New Zealand residential architecture ever since people first arrived here. One could say that, in regards to our houses at least, we've always trodden rather lightly on the land, not that we were following some environmentally conscious path. (If God hadn't meant us to live in wooden houses, why did He give us all those beautiful native trees?) But although our history is built from wood, the timber tradition is rather paradoxical: it speaks of transience as well as settlement. As Auckland architect Pip Cheshire has put it, 'We're still pulling the packing cases up above the high water mark.' (*Urbis Design Annual*, 2003). Cheshire might have been talking about the architecture of Auckland in particular, but the point seems to have general application to settler New Zealand. Perhaps a certain architectural flimsiness is only to be expected of a migrant nation at the end

of the world; our national anthem, one occasionally thinks, shouldn't be 'God Defend New Zealand'. More honestly, it might be 'Should I Stay, or Should I Go'?

Visitors, too, have often remarked on the character of New Zealand housing, being variously charmed or appalled by its ephemerality. Coming from Cape Town, 'a city of brickwork and masonry', Lance Herbst found New Zealand's 'world of lightweight' liberating. For a while, he says, 'it was a question of how light can we go?' (*Architecture New Zealand*, January/February 2003). Herbst Architects has pursued this interest in levity — not to be confused with insubstantiality — in their Great Barrier Island baches. (The practice is now designing its sixth bach on the same Great Barrier beach.) The client for this beach house was familiar with both the island and Herbst Architects' work. 'He came to us and said, "Do what you do",' Lance Herbst says. The client did not want 'a mansion on the beach — something that screamed out opulence', and that's one reason, Herbst says, along with a programmatic response to site, a diagnosis of the nature of holiday architecture, and the observance of height-to-boundary regulations, that the house is split into several elements. This formal separation has allowed for a modesty of scale; after all, as Herbst says, 'It is a beach house!'

Construction is expensive on remote Great Barrier, but an uncompromising client gave the architects generous scope to demonstrate, with the help of able builders, their mastery of detailing and skill with materials. The budget enabled Herbst Architects to realise an expressive architecture of timber and stainless steel: the house is bonded by steel plates, pins and bolts

1 workshop
2 boat shed
3 bedroom
4 bathroom
5 covered deck
6 dining
7 kitchen
8 living

— a thousand of them. A method of assembly combining strength and lightness means the house is both pushed apart and held together. (The plan itself expresses this equilibrium between separation and connection, with the central gabion wall acting as a fulcrum.) An accretion of material layers imparts refinement and encourages legibility, although the bach is no quick and easy holiday read. Nicky Herbst talks of the house's 'slow release of experiences'. Perhaps one could also interpret its layers of materials as levels of meaning, or even, as in some arcane discipline — high diving, or performing on the parallel bars — as degrees of difficulty. These might seem fanciful comparisons, but the Lindale Bach is a work that clearly reveals the evidence of challenges sought in order to be artfully overcome.

While the architects have put the bones of the house on display they were also able to, as Lance Herbst says, 'explore the nature of the skin'. This is a real concern to Herbst, as the very lightness that he finds compelling in local architecture is now being compromised by mandated building practices. In response to the recent 'leaky building crisis' New Zealand buildings, Herbst says, 'are becoming dense and heavy, bogged down with waterproofing'. Forget floating; they're starting to look as though they can't even breathe through their thick and often lumpy skins. In this house, though, the architects have separated the 'wet' elements — that is, those that can get wet — from those that must remain dry.

The Lindale Bach, in a real sense, is built on an understanding of the way people behave on holiday, at the beach. There's a little behavioural guidance on offer, as well. In the design, the architects have taken account of what they describe as 'holiday rituals'. For example, the fishing trip is a quotidian occurrence on Great Barrier: out in the morning, back late in the afternoon. So the south-west deck — one of two roofed decks offering alternative shelter from the winds coming off the sea to the front and the mountain behind — is proximate to the drive, and ready to receive the catch of the day. The architects are firm in their conviction that bach life is lived outside. There is one 'almost winter' communal space in the Lindale Bach — the living area — and even that is sunken so as not to hinder through-views from the rear deck. 'People just gravitate to the outside,' Nicky Herbst says (well, yes; with these decks, they would).

For the Herbsts — and, presumably, for their client — a holiday at a beach, especially at a beach on Great Barrier, is not a comfortable blob-out surrounded by all mod-cons. The preservation of the 'rituals' of holiday life — the regular 'events', whether they be swimming or showering, fishing or cooking, that provide the daily rhythms of a vacation — entails a sacrifice of convenience. Lance Herbst puts it more strongly: 'Convenience robs a holiday of its rituals.' The architects are not quite as prescriptive as they once were in their attitude to comfort and amenity — 'Now we at least provide cover when you're going from the living room to the bathroom' — but they still ensure that holidaymakers on Great Barrier are aware of the preciousness of the island's resources. 'Out on Great Barrier,' Lance Herbst says, 'we under-light our buildings. If you want more light, use the Coleman.' One way or another, you *will* have beach experiences at the Lindale Bach.

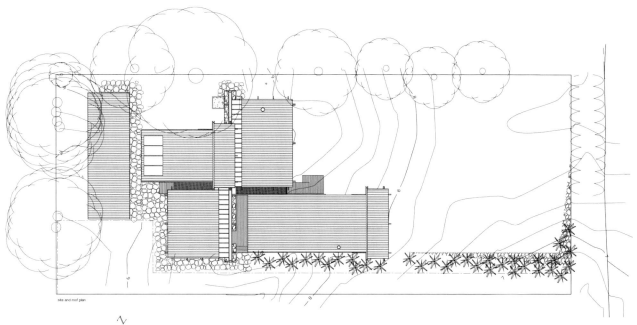

site and roof plan

SITE PLAN

The bach, showing the main
bedroom designed to peek
over the dunes to the ocean,
with photo-voltaic solar panels
on the roof above.

Right: View of the bach from the east, showing the repeated forms of the main structures.

Above: Eaves provide shading and conceal the collection of potable rain water.

Left: Cedar cladding, showing the external structure of the sliding doors.

Above: The living area, on the seaward side of the house, is lowered to allow views through from the dining and kitchen areas.

Right: Looking through the kitchen to the gabion spine. The bench at right provides open storage.

Above left: Bathroom.

Above: Rear covered deck.

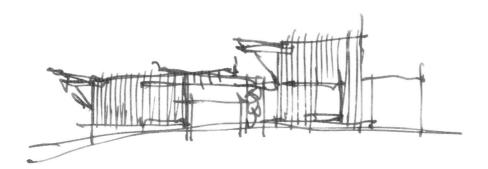

Above: Front deck.

Right: Looking from the front deck into the kitchen.

Facing page: The rear building is set back from the gabion wall to admit light into the bathroom.

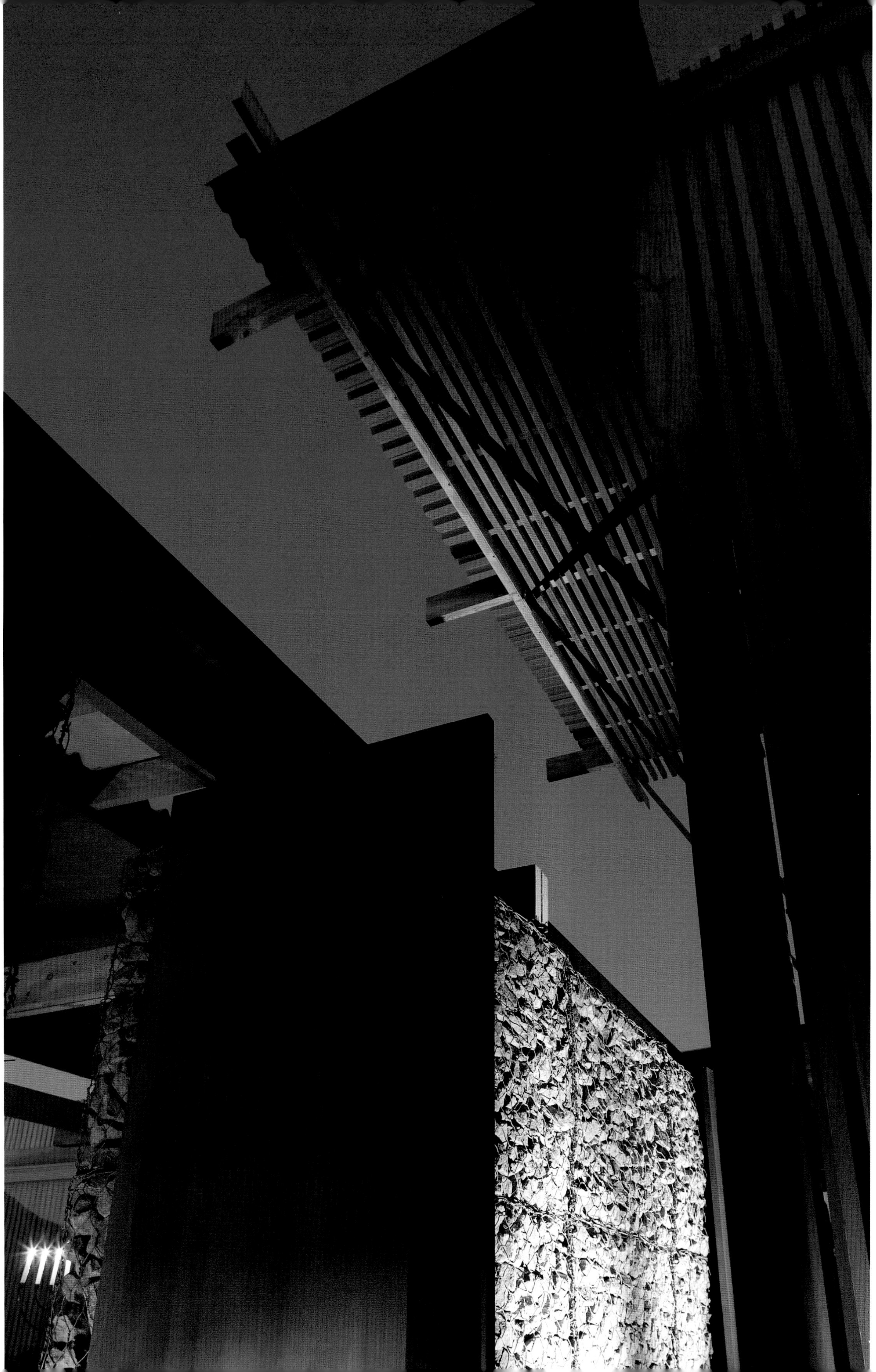

WAKATIPU BASIN HOUSE

4

FEARON HAY
ARCHITECTS

CENTRAL OTAGO

2005

Previous spread: View of the
Wakatipu Basin House, looking
through the sculptural work on
the front terrace.

IN WHICH THE AUCKLAND adepts of the modern pavilion seek to adapt to a harsher clime, and thereby demonstrate that they are not just fair-weather designers at home on northern littorals. That is, Fearon Hay head for the Southern Alps, and on a site outside Queenstown tough it out against winter cold, summer heat, prevailing winds and the most majestic scenery in New Zealand. The Wakatipu Basin House is an architectural statement — an over-used term which, in this case, actually has some meaning. It's not just that the house, in its form and materials, has a deliberately sculptural character; more than that, what the architects are saying is that they can make a long, flat-roofed building work in an alpine basin.

There is something of a Central Otago tradition of provocative architecture (as distinct from shameless buildings, in which Queenstown, especially, abounds). One could say that proximity to the sublime stirs ambition, but architects must build, and must figure out a response to the context in which they build. That response could be referential or reverential, or it could be more assertive. Some architects have obviously decided that the best way to react to a formidable topography is to stand up to it. John Blair, for example, by now a veteran architect of the region, was designing bold object-houses in Central Otago 30 years ago. Two notable examples of his early-career work are near-neighbours at Dalefield. The Sanders House (1975) is a boxy building with a verticality made more pronounced by its elevated site — locals reportedly called it 'the lighthouse'. The Tennent House (1978) is a two-level but more horizontal form with a steep-pitched roof and a large, landscape-framing void in the middle of the building at ground level. When designing against the monumental backdrops of Central Otago, Blair has sought to achieve what he has described as 'a balance of strengths'. (Peter Shaw, *A History of New Zealand Architecture*, 2003.)

In architecture, as in most areas of human activity — art, politics, stand-up comedy — there is a difference between provocation and inappropriateness. Architects tend to applaud the former (it's kind of risqué) and regret the latter (it's rather off-colour). It's true, the difference is not always clear-cut, and is often a matter of subjective judgment; what stops the stimulating being dismissed as the shocking is performance. Delight is a matter of taste, not so firmness and commodity. Blair, perhaps, would say that there's no question that his Central Otago houses, though declarative, are appropriate. They work, don't they?

What of Fearon Hay's Wakatipu Basin House? This is both an admired and, locally, a somewhat controversial house. (Its celebrity wouldn't be possible without its visibility; unlike much of the top-shelf residential architecture of Central Otago, the house can be seen from a public road.) There seems to be some debate about the building's belonging, which is probably no surprise to Jeff Fearon and Tim Hay, who are well aware of the discussions of the regional typologies of Central Otago. Indeed, the design for the house could be said to have anticipated criticism of its, yes, appropriateness. Fearon says he knew that the house, on its flat site, would be seen from numerous vantage points, and intended that from a distance it should register as a rural building.

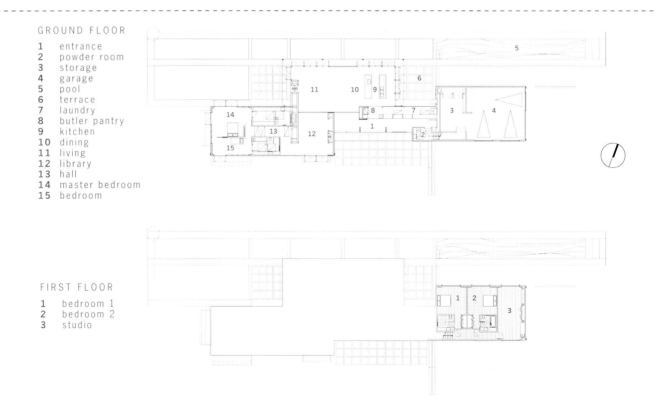

GROUND FLOOR

1 entrance
2 powder room
3 storage
4 garage
5 pool
6 terrace
7 laundry
8 butler pantry
9 kitchen
10 dining
11 living
12 library
13 hall
14 master bedroom
15 bedroom

FIRST FLOOR

1 bedroom 1
2 bedroom 2
3 studio

He says, too, that the design is consciously a reaction against the 'American lodge and ranch-style' development proliferating across the Wakatipu Basin. (One can't help fearing for the future of this tough and tender landscape: its destiny could easily be suburban.)

So, the language of the house's design is intended to be expressed with a rural vernacular inflection. Whether this design dialect is local or not, it is certainly distinctive; with its grey zinc cladding, this is one staunch-looking house. It's possible to interpret it as the product of an Otago-Auckland entente, but one that is not all that cordiale: a big, bad shed seems to be having its way with a visiting pavilion. A load of old bull? Some local architects are not convinced that this is the right house for this site. The issues are not merely aesthetic, although, with a practice so conscious of the gaze it is difficult to separate aesthetic from other concerns. There are the questions of the roof — its flatness, that is, in a snow zone — and the eaves and overhangs — their absence, that is, from a house on such an exposed site.

No doubt this house is engineered and detailed to withstand the elements — its firmness should not be in question — but it is interesting to contrast the strategy followed here with that recently pursued by another architect on another flat, if more modest, site in the Wakatipu Basin. The Clarke House was designed by Max Wild, an architect who has lived in Arrowtown for nearly 20 years. It, too, is 'an object in a green field', as Wild puts it (*Architecture New Zealand*, May/June 2006), but one that is more obviously tethered to its site. The Clarke House expresses a conciliatory approach to its environment: the pitched roof is pulled down low, the verandah is deep, the rooms recede into the interior. Wild's is an architecture of gentle transitions, combining dedicated and 'indeterminate' or 'left-over' spaces, a deliberate blurring of the programme that is subversive of the notion of the architect as boss of space.

In contrast, Fearon Hay are masters of clarity. They have to be; big budgets, prime sites, demanding clients — things could easily get out of hand if order wasn't maintained. The tethering that occurs in Fearon Hay houses tends to be internal. Functional elements, often treated as sculptural pieces, serve as spatial foci or anchors: big concrete tables in the Butler House in Westmere, for example, and, in this house, the fireplace in the living room that continues through into the library. John Blair's search for 'a balance of strengths' seems apposite here: surely all architecture in the Wakatipu Basin is a struggle against entropy? For, really, it's all about the view.

The Wakatipu Basin House, positioned on an east-west axis, with a long apron of terrace and a long, tall, run of glazing on the north elevation is sited to take maximum advantage of a dizzying array of vistas. What a topographical cast: Coronet Peak to the north; The Remarkables to the south; the Crown Range to the east; Mt Dewar to the north-west (not forgetting the Shotover River, just to the west). Faced with nature so deployed, it's no wonder Fearon Hay chose to suit up this house in metal armour. Did the inspiration for this house really come from vernacular architecture? Or did it come from classic literature? The Wakatipu Basin House doesn't so much suggest the shed as invoke the spirit of Don Quixote.

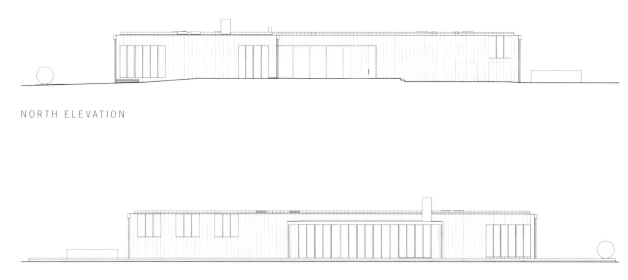

NORTH ELEVATION

SOUTH ELEVATION

View along main terrace
showing the phalanx of steel
French doors.

Above: Entrance, with the living area at right.

Right: The living area, which gives out to the main terrace.

Facing page, top: View from the main terrace through the house towards The Remarkables.

Facing page, lower: View from the kitchen and dining areas to Coronet Peak.

View from the living area
towards Coronet Peak.

South elevation, with the
bedroom/studio wing to
the left, the living area in
the centre, and the master
bedroom to the right.

RETREAT

VERNON

5

MALCOLM WALKER
ARCHITECTS

AOTEA HARBOUR,
WAIKATO

2006

THIS IS NOT A bach for softies. For starters, the little house — just one bedroom, with another in the shed/sleepout — is located on the North Island's west and wilder coast. To say it's on the edge of nowhere would be a city-centric slight, but to say it's on a promontory above Aotea Harbour wouldn't mean much to most people. The house is reached by choosing correctly among the various gravel and dirt roading options on offer in the hilly country between Raglan and Kawhia. According to temperament, drivers, as they go in and out of cellphone range, will be reassured or unsettled by the knowledge that in the twenty-first century, a couple of hours from Auckland, it's perfectly possible to get lost in New Zealand.

In this district a dot on a map is more likely to indicate a marae than a village — most settlements are well and truly lapsed. As well as signs of long and continued Maori occupation, the land provides plenty of evidence of the effects of post-settlement farming. Hillsides are eroded, and once-cleared pastures are reverting to bush. In sum, without wishing to exaggerate the region's wildness and remoteness, or the weight of its historical freight, this is a challenging locale for the holiday-home owner. Some personal, as well as structural resilience is called for.

The clients who engaged Malcolm Walker to design this 'retreat' both grew up on farms in the area. They know how to make do, fix things, get by. (Importantly, they know the local pig-hunter, who will come and deal with the feral porkers that ruck up the land above the house.)

On the site they chose for their house — the most accessible of several promontories on their steep, 20-hectare block — they knew that the price of a prospect across Aotea Harbour was regular confrontation with the elements. The full implications of this trade-off were made apparent during construction, when the house's half-built, central block wall was blown over.

The house faces to the south-west, across to the village of Aotea and the bar that obstructs the entrance to the tidal harbour. It occupies the sort of position favoured by Maori for pa sites up and down New Zealand's coastline. Perched on the only visible bit of levelled land, clad in lightweight Zincalume, the house seems to advertise its ephemerality. Thin-skinned, all alone, up against greatly superior forces — it's not surprising that the house has been likened to 'a tin dinghy on a wild sea'.

Positioned for views, the house with its inhabitants is, of course, also in the view, although a paradox begs some consideration: Can you be exposed if there's no-one to see you? Any observers of the Vernon house would have to be out to sea, or off the beaten track. The long odds against voyeurism, however, did not convince the clients to accept their architect's suggestion of a floor-to-ceiling window next to the shower. They also passed on the proposition that the house be painted black. This may have made the house less obvious, but the clients thought it may also have made it more 'ominous'. In an isolated location, perhaps it's better to come clean.

There is a more important point to be made about being on show. In some parts of New Zealand

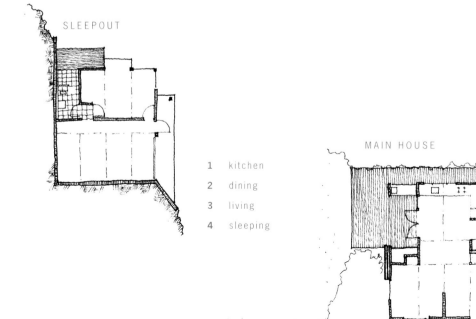

SLEEPOUT

MAIN HOUSE

N

1 kitchen
2 dining
3 living
4 sleeping

a holiday home is a graphic expression of social inequality. Even if the 'bach' is a modest building, it is still a luxury: a dwelling occupied only occasionally by owners from elsewhere. Anywhere in the world such evident disparity between the haves and have-nots, or the mobile and the stuck, can chafe. In the new bach-lands both outsiders and locals must contemplate, now and then and not necessarily fearfully or maliciously, the correctives available to people who are there all of the time.

The Vernon Retreat might be obvious but it is certainly not ostentatious. 'A simple farmhouse on a hill' is Malcolm Walker's summation of the design imagery — a description that is typically understated, but well short of the whole story. Two gable forms are used — so far, so country — but, separated by a section of flat roof, they are staggered to provide a small deck on the south side and an enclosed porch on the north.

The interior layout separates the rooms that are private (the bedroom and bathroom) from those that are more social (kitchen, dining and living). A bed-sitting area, at the opposite diagonal to the bedroom, might have been partially screened off, if the architect had his way (he mostly did).

In a house that's already small there may be no point in further constricting movement, but that doesn't mean surrendering order. Without breaking up the space in the 'public' part of the house, Walker does just enough to convey spatial purpose: functional differentiation, without overt delineation. And, while he was asked to produce a building that would be

simple and easy to maintain, he hasn't over-indulged in austerity (the deep window-seats on the west side solicit long afternoon naps).

As always, this architect has designed a house from the inside out, one that's smart and sufficient, and comfortable in its raw skin.

The house has a prime prospect across the tidal Aotea Harbour.

South elevation, with the
sleepout at right.

Tin boat with zinc house.

Above left: Living area with
multi-function daybeds.

Above: View to the entrance
of Aotea Harbour from the
living area.

Left: Dining room, showing the
open-plan nature of the design.

Right: Looking over the house to the harbour entrance.

Facing page: The entrance on the north side serves as a country-style covered porch.

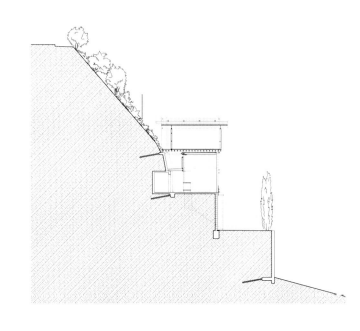

ORIENTALBAYHOUSE

6

ARCHITECTURE
WORKSHOP

WELLINGTON

2005

6

WHAT HAVE WE GOT here? A ziggurat of cubed forms stepping down Mt Victoria, a tall glazed pavilion tacked to the hillside, and a couple of vaulted wooden cabins that could be anchorite outstations of St Gerard's Monastery, the Wellington landmark up the road. A family house, in other words — and one of the most audacious experiments in New Zealand residential architecture in a generation.

The Oriental Bay House is many things, among them a testament to its architect's talent and his family's patience. It's an exercise in sufficiency, an attempt to answer the question: how much structure is really necessary? It's a rebuttal of the familiar architectural defence of diminished responsibility (the client/council/budget made me do it). It's an affront to the orientational norms of Oriental Bay — schizophrenically, half the house seems to pretend that the view doesn't matter, while the other half suggests it's all that matters. It's a demonstration of Hibernian contrariness staged in one of New Zealand's most privileged neighbourhoods. (Or, as the Redemptorist Fathers of St Gerard's might have put it, an assertion of free will against the claims of predestination.) It's a series of propositions that may have set off in the general direction of a conclusion, but got diverted along the way. It's clever, knowing and seriously playful; measuring it against most New Zealand residential architecture is like putting a Tom Stoppard play up against an episode of *Shortland Street*.

Chris Kelly has been at work on this house, on and off, for almost 15 years; for his children, if not their visiting friends, the house is normal. (When his young daughter was asked by her teacher to draw her house, she drew a picture of people living on a platform.) In its duration, situation and expository nature, if not in its size or shape, the project has some resemblance to the very model of Wellington work-in-progress architecture: Ian Athfield's own house, spilling like a Cycladic village down a hill on the other side of the harbour. As does the Athfield House, this house requires that occupants and visitors keep their wits about them — there are stairs to edge up, balconies to balance on, voids to leap over. (Architecture can be a risky business — at home Athfield once impaled himself on a steel reinforcing bar.)

Perhaps it's not surprising that the Oriental Bay House exhibits some of the chutzpah of the Athfield House: Kelly spent the first five years of his career with Athfield's practice. That, though, was just the start of his post-graduate education. With his wife, Ann Clifford, Kelly went to England in the 1980s, and worked for the eminent modernist Denys Lasdun before studying under the radical practitioner and theoretician Peter Cook in Frankfurt. Back in London, he got a job with Ian Ritchie, a distinguished architect who, Kelly says, had left Foster's (Foster's!) because he considered a project to have been compromised. Then, the best break of all: a position with international 'star architect' Renzo Piano. Kelly was a senior designer on Piano's Kansai Airport project in Osaka; later, at the end of the 1990s, he was co-leader of Piano's Sydney office for the design and construction of Aurora Tower. That's quite a CV, in anyone's terms, and quite a lot of intellectual firepower to bring to bear on 400 square metres of Wellington hillside.

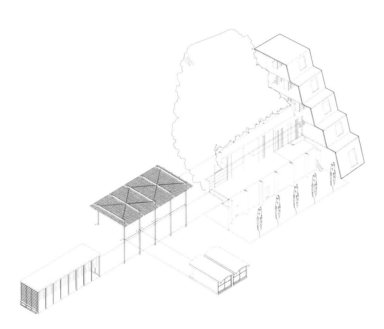

Most new housing is simply the cost-governed development of a plot of land. If an architect is involved, some consideration will have been given to a building's relationship to the section on which it sits, or at least to the provision of 'indoor–outdoor flow'. In one case, the land is just left over; in the other, it's a lifestyle supplement. When he planned his house, Kelly says, his approach was to treat the whole site 'as a constructed environment'. The idea is that 'you're living on the whole piece of land'. The house makes a case for free-range architecture, at a time when much urban housing seems to be modelled on battery farming.

Interpreting the site as a whole does not mean that the landscape or the architecture is amorphous. There are, Kelly says, three different landscapes on the site: 'a formal garden' — a flat lawn, surely unique on Mt Victoria, that allows space for a run-up (if the bowling is slow) and room for drives (as long as they're straight); an 'outdoor room' — a pavilion, that is; and the 'Garden of Gethsemene' — the scrubby slope behind the house, steep enough to drive the staunchest architect to existential doubt. And there are two main structures, so different as to be opposites: the 'cave' — the stepped building on the site's southern boundary; and the 'tent' — the glazed pavilion that looks over Oriental Parade and across the harbour to Tinakori Hill.

Kelly is a contrapuntist and this house exemplifies his practice of juxtaposing solid and light building elements. He says he always intended that the house would have two main parts, and that they would complement each other. But there is so much typological distance between the buildings, and so much

temporal separation (the 'cave' was occupied in 1997; the 'tent' in 2005), that it's no wonder the project caused puzzlement. When the pavilion went up, Kelly says, 'People said "you must have been annoyed when the neighbour built so close to you".' That sort of comment was nothing on the response to the earlier structure. 'The stepped-down form disturbs people,' Kelly says. Why? It's the small windows: an understandable desire to safeguard privacy gets taken for an insolent renunciation of prospect. Rewi Thompson's own back-to-the-view house in Auckland (1985) prompted a similar reaction, Kelly says: 'It's a bit "sod you".'

Well, Kelly might say, if it's glazing people wanted to gaze at, he's certainly given it to them now. The pavilion presents a long, high wall of windows to the promenaders on Oriental Parade. Kelly was interested in answering the question: 'How little could you do to live in a garden?' More than he wanted, perhaps; ephemerality had to be reconciled with practicality. This room for lounging, cooking and dining is so big that the family, who had been living on three floors in the 'cave', thought 'we'd inherited a fortune'. They had inherited a retaining wall which, in its extant state, now serves as the pavilion's rear wall (rendering other renditions of that familiar gesture, the exterior wall brought indoors, fairly contrived). To the builder's embarrassment, Kelly says, the pavilion has minimal interior linings; a shoji screen was to go against the north wall — 'but you can change your mind'. There are still things to do in this house — plenty of opportunities for further changes of mind. 'You could live in this house a few ways,' Kelly says. So you could, if you were up for it.

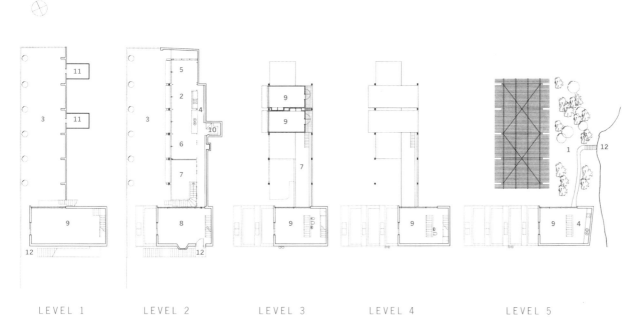

1 wild wind garden
2 outdoor room
3 formal garden
4 kitchen
5 day living
6 dining
7 terrace
8 night living
9 sleep/live/work
10 pantry
11 store
12 entry

LEVEL 1   LEVEL 2   LEVEL 3   LEVEL 4   LEVEL 5

External passage to top-level
bedrooms; Oriental Bay and its
fountain beyond.

Above: One of the two vaulted
bedrooms perched above the
living pavilion.

Left: Looking from the pavilion
kitchen across the dining area
to the harbour.

Right: Looking across the double-height living pavilion.

Below right: Passage between the two forms, showing the existing concrete retaining wall that serves as the rear wall of the kitchen.

Facing page: The translucent, timber-framed end wall of the pavilion, with steel framing.

Looking past the 'cave' to the pavilion.

Above left: The exposed
structure and simple
furnishings of the pavilion.

Above: Kitchen, showing the
patina of the old retaining wall.

Left: The house in its Oriental
Bay context.

HUDSON–YOUNGHOUSE

7

GUY TARRANT
COOK SARGISSON
TARRANT & PIRIE

WAIHEKE ISLAND

2006

WE KNOW WAIHEKE ISLAND is a real estate agent's wet dream but sociologists must be quite fond of it as well. It can't be that often that they see a class system recrudescing in real time. For decades Waiheke was sufficiently remote from Auckland and sufficiently deprived of infrastructure to function as a retreat for those rich in time and low on income. Looking back — not far back — Waiheke was a fool's paradise: there was no way that a largish island near the country's biggest city was going to be allowed to rest in peace. It wasn't that it would be pressed into production, the presence of a number of boutique wineries nothwistanding: the land, once the ferries got faster, was too valuable for that. But Waiheke is being appropriated; the island is becoming a bourgeois plantation. What's developing on Waiheke is the hegemony of the modern leisure class.

As always, class and architectural hegemony go together. Houses on Waiheke used to be as informal as their inhabitants; the whole place was an adhocracy. Now, architecture announces itself even before the ferry has docked. The big houses on the hills above Matiatia wharf are forerunners of the holiday homes to come. The new architecture that commands the heights and claims the coast on Waiheke is often, wittingly or carelessly, very assertive. Locals, when they encounter it, might get some inkling of what it must have been like for an Anglo-Saxon villager confronted by a Norman keep, or an Irish peasant by an English manor house. The stonking housing around Matiatia, it's the architecture of occupation.

The holiday house that Guy Tarrant has designed for a site above Onetangi Beach, on the north side of Waiheke, is not in the same seigneurial league as some of the recent architect-designed houses on the island. On its patch, though, it's certainly dominant. The Hudson-Young House, a boxed stack of two rectilinear storeys on a garage base, thrusts upwards and outwards from its platform atop a steep drive. This is one building that really is an erection; the cantilever is especially impressive, its thrust made more pronounced by the angle of the incline beneath. Anyone viewing the house from the street below would have to wonder: how does it keep it up?

Strict discipline is the answer. This is a very controlled design: ordered, focused, and rational — not qualities traditionally associated with Waiheke, or with New Zealand holiday architecture. It's a fine exemplar of that contemporary type: the holiday house as anti-bach. Tarrant, one suspects, is not an architect who has much sympathy with extemporisation — 'I don't like fussy things' — nor one who has to be exhorted to get with the programme. The plan's the thing for Tarrant. It drives the design of the Hudson-Young House, while the steel portal structural system — a system deployed in the 1950s and 1960s with such casual elegance by the Southern Californian modernist Craig Ellwood — organizes the space. (Tarrant, and he's hardly alone in this, is an admirer of Ellwood, a cool charmer who fused Los Angeles style and International Style.)

With plan and structure locked in sync, the Hudson-Young House marches along to a regular modular beat: on both upper floors, three bays each 6.2 metres long and virtually square, and then a half-

Previous spread: North elevation of the Hudson–Young House, looking down the curve of Onetangi Beach.

Far right: Covered terraces are cantilevered out from the main structure.

Following spread, left: Upper-level covered terrace off the main bedroom, with bath and moveable louvered screens.

Following spread, right: Front elevation.

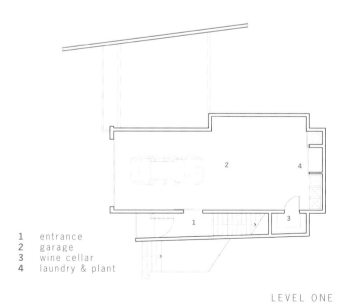

1 entrance
2 garage
3 wine cellar
4 laundry & plant

LEVEL ONE

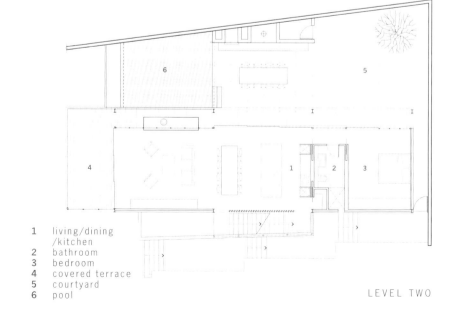

1 living/dining
   /kitchen
2 bathroom
3 bedroom
4 covered terrace
5 courtyard
6 pool

LEVEL TWO

bay front balcony. There's even some vertical, as well as lateral repetition; a third-floor bay with a bathroom and bedroom sits on top of a similarly organised second-floor bay. 'You get a sense of where everything is,' Tarrant says. 'Some might not find that so interesting, but I quite like it.' Tarrant's description of the house as both rational and relaxed seems contradictory, but the logic of the layout does have a soothing effect. Visitors to a holiday house might quite like to be spared the deductive challenge presented by the old Kiwi bach or beach house, in which a search for a loo meant a grope in the dark, and so, quite likely, did a hunt for a bed.

The rectilinearity of the house is not experienced as a pinched occupation of space, in significant part because Tarrant has located the stairwell in a translucent container against the south wall. This makes sense — the south side was not wanted for anything else, such as a view in that direction — but it's an eloquent as well as a pragmatic gesture. Light is brought into the central module on both accommodation floors, and the glazed north side of the box offers a prospect of Onetangi Beach.

Yes, the beach: the point of it all. Like all elevated coastal houses, the Hudson-Young House is, as Tarrant acknowledges, 'a viewing platform'. Without wishing to be coarsely reductive, a project such as this house is a series of relatively expensive machinations to get a few people, plus drinks, into a position where they can comfortably and loftily contemplate a maritime sunset. The architect ultimately has to deliver the view, and in this case Tarrant has lined it up and bagged it; the upper floors of the house are ranged like long gun barrels right

down the line where the sea meets the sand on Onetangi Beach. Two floors means two goes at this western view, but Tarrant says the house was destined, anyway, to be double height, or rather triple height. There was quite a lot of house to be fitted onto a section subject to local restrictions on site coverage (on Waiheke allowance must be made for waste disposal and permeable areas). Smaller footprint, therefore taller building.

Tarrant would have preferred to position the house further to the unfavoured south of the site, but couldn't buck the height-to-boundary regulations without the neighbour's permission. As it is, the house must contend with some strategic imbalance: an excess of *lebensraum* on the southern border. The building is all wall on this side — protection not connection is the goal — therefore the land seems left over. It would have been of more use on the north side of the house, added to the sheltered and soon to be ivy-covered courtyard which is the locus of outdoor living. Well, no architectural project is realised without compromise.

The Hudson-Young House is a view house, and therefore an exposed house. A bank to the east covers its rear; the south elevation is closed; leaving the western and northern fronts open to bright sunlight and public, or at least, neighbourly gaze. In response, Tarrant has devised a system of adjustable louvred screens that offer a formidable range of shading options. The permutations must almost be endless; is this architecture as elaborate fan dance? No, too whimsical. It's architecture as choreography: planned, efficient, and all worked out. Rumpty old Waiheke is learning some classy new moves.

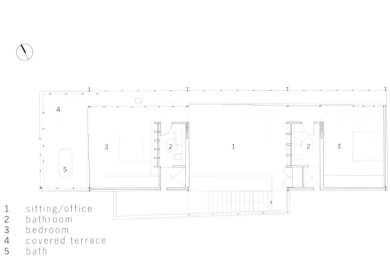

1 sitting/office
2 bathroom
3 bedroom
4 covered terrace
5 bath

LEVEL THREE

Above: Looking over the kitchen island to the stairs in the translucent glazed box on the south side of the house.

Far left: Stair detail, showing the angled timber screen.

Left: Upper-level bathroom.

Facing page, top: Circulation space on the upper level, showing sliding, glazed walls, with louvered sunscreens beyond.

Facing page, lower: Looking from the dining area on the main floor into the courtyard.

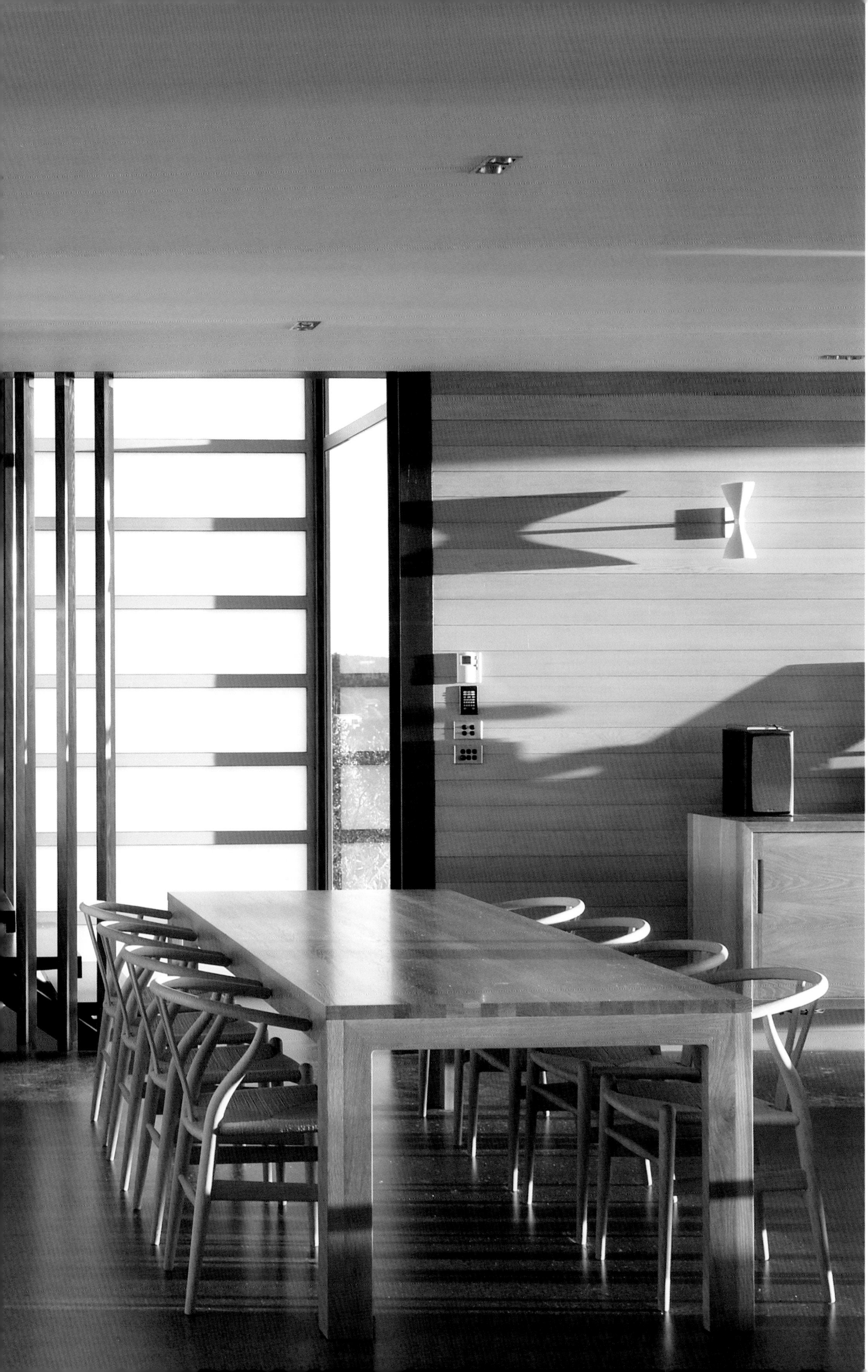

The setting sun pours into the main level of the house.

Facing page: Looking down
the north elevation.

Left: The lantern on the south
side of the house's stairwell.

McCAHONHOUSE

8

PETE BOSSLEY
ARCHITECTS

TITIRANGI

2006

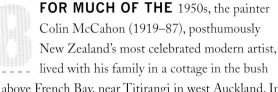

Previous spread: View from the entry boardwalk to the main living area of the McCahon House.

FOR MUCH OF THE 1950s, the painter Colin McCahon (1919–87), posthumously New Zealand's most celebrated modern artist, lived with his family in a cottage in the bush above French Bay, near Titirangi in west Auckland. In those days, life out west could be rudimentary, but at least it wasn't suburban. Free and feral, Titirangi was Auckland's bohemian frontier.

In that environment, McCahon was almost bourgeois. True, he was an artist, but he had a wife, four children and a day job (at the Auckland Art Gallery). And a house, too, in a place where many structures were hilariously reductive. Bach? Luxury. At French Bay people holidayed in car packing cases dragged into the bush. But while the McCahon cottage was recognisably a dwelling, its simplicity would now seem shocking. Even in its current state, restored and repurposed by architects Graeme Burgess and Rick Pearson as a visitor centre illustrating the artist's French Bay years (1953–60), the house incites disbelief. How could it have contained six people? One answer is that it didn't, not fully: the two south-facing bedrooms in the basement are both one wall short of a full set — the outside wall, that is. In one of the bedrooms, the built-in bunks are still there; on a wet winter's day, it's impossible not to shiver at the sight.

Decades after McCahon had left French Bay, the cottage, the garage where he painted, and some surrounding land were bought by Waitakere City Council and gifted to the McCahon House Trust. Any temptation to treat the old cottage as a shrine was resisted, with reason — McCahon may have had religious inclinations, but he was no saint. Instead,

says McCahon House Trust manager Cynthia Smith, discussion turned to coupling a restoration job with a 'living project' on the same site. The trust raised funds for a building that would provide accommodation and a studio for mid-career artists and took its brief for the McCahon Residency — for 'something that would not overshadow the cottage, but would not be overshadowed by it' — to architect Pete Bossley.

The choice of a designer for this project was, in many ways, a matter of natural selection. Want a house? Bossley is one of New Zealand's most acclaimed residential architects. Prefer some experience with cultural commissions? Bossley, when he was at Jasmax, was co-designer of Te Papa, New Zealand's national museum (1997). Like some understanding of the artistic productive process? Drawing is an obsession for Bossley, one of those increasingly rare architects who thinks with a pencil. Require a sophisticated understanding of the relationship between building and landscape? Bossley, by now, has an extensive portfolio of projects, many of them houses for wealthy clients privileged to own beautiful sites, in which he has sought to balance the demands of occupiers with the more muted claims of the natural environment. Comfortable on the coast, Bossley has shown he's also quite at home in the bush.

There were other qualities Bossley brought to this job. Most importantly, he was up for it. As the trust recognised, the new neighbour to the historic cottage would have to be a strong but sensitive type: respectful, but not easily over-awed. Bossley has exhibited a fair amount of courage and grace in his career; for example, he survived the Te Papa controversy with his confidence intact. Lesser

spirits may have sunk beneath the small society diatribes directed against Te Papa and its designers, but Bossley has remained open and generous, and unafraid to confront the obscurantism prevalent in any public discussion of architecture in New Zealand.

In the design of the McCahon Residency a sense of levity was also appropriate. For one thing, the legacy of McCahon is heavy enough, and for another, the physical environment at French Bay is rather intense: very green and close and, especially in winter, often dour. There were also site-specific reasons to tread lightly. The residency stands on and projects from a steep slope, amid regenerating forest — an impressive cast of indigenous species starring dozens of protected kauri trees. (Lime-haters: this is no place for a big concrete platform.)

Bossley has sufficiently distanced the 'living project' from the existing cottage to allow both some breathing space. The residence is a Y-shaped arrangement of forms spun off a kitchen/dining core. There are two bedroom wings — the second bedroom is a recognition that by mid-career artists have usually accumulated a family — and a living area. Picking its way among the kauri, the residency is a house among trees, whereas the separate studio is more obviously a tree house. It's not that the studio doesn't have visible means of support; it's just that its steel legs seem improbably spindly. Architecture being one long protest against gravity, it's not surprising that architects love to cantilever (it's the next best thing to levitation) and this studio might be the closest Bossley has come to achieving weightlessness. The soaring effect would have been even more pronounced if Bossley's

design for a narrow walkway projecting from the studio out into the trees had been realised.

The McCahon Residency is really an anti-McCahon cottage. Where the cottage is squat and tight, the residence is loose and light. Bossley has tried to make the most of the light that is available on the south side of a bush-clad hill. Two of the walls in the living area and the bedrooms are floor-to-ceiling windows — the trees are right there — and a large skylight is cut into the ceiling above the kitchen/dining area that is the building's fulcrum. (The glass is strong enough to resist kauri drop; the male cones bounce, the females explode.) An enthusiasm for material diversity has always characterised Bossley's architecture — he is impatient with talk of material 'honesty', once a central tenet of modernism but now a tired excuse for lack of imagination — and in the McCahon Residence he has mixed and matched glass, steel, mesh, wood, board and black PVC downpiping. Bossley has also never been po-faced about colour; here, interior and exterior panels of yellow and red not only signify an artists' residence but also counter French Bay cafard. 'You need some vibrancy in Titirangi,' says Cynthia Smith.

Bossley's partiality for expressive materials and colours is most apparent in the sheets of rusted steel cladding on the north side of the studio. The architect had to fight to retain this element, and the clients are now glad that he did. The steel wall — an artwork, really — typifies a building that Bossley says is less a house than 'an experience'. The architect has dealt convincingly with the legacies attached to this site; now it's up to artists to rise to the challenge.

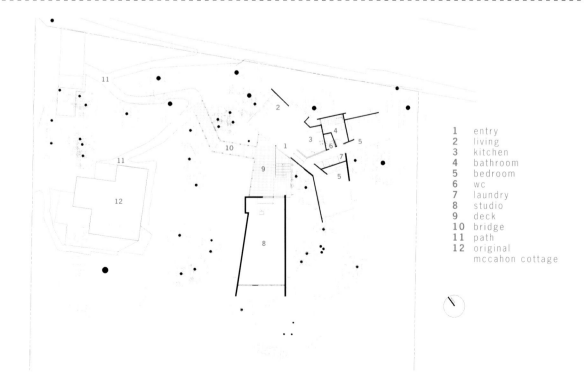

1	entry
2	living
3	kitchen
4	bathroom
5	bedroom
6	wc
7	laundry
8	studio
9	deck
10	bridge
11	path
12	original mccahon cottage

Deck between the house and the artist's studio, looking to the main entrance and dining room.

Above: Looking from the dining into the living area.

Left: Front door and main entrance. A skylight admits light into the kitchen/dining area.

Dining area and kitchen, with
skylight above. The glass is
strengthened against
kauri drop.

Above: The artist's studio.

Left: The rusted steel wall
of the studio seen through
native bush.

Facing page: Looking through
the second bedroom.

Above: The main bedroom.

Left: Joinery detail.

The house and studio in their bush setting.

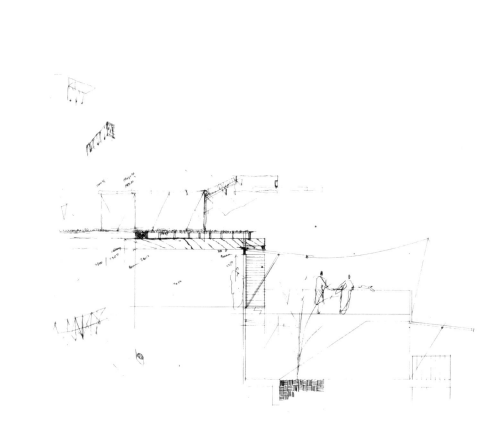

NORTHSHOREHOUSE

9

ARCHITECTUS

DEVONPORT,
AUCKLAND

2002

THERE'S AN IMPERTURBABILITY TO

this house, but also a hint of tension. Both dug into and stretched along its narrow site looking over Ngataringa Bay, the house seems poised between settlement and departure. Not flight: the motion the house implies is the deliberate and stately progress of an ocean liner slipping its moorings. This reading is encouraged by the house's waterside situation, and also by the uninterrupted view of its long western elevation available from the neighbouring reserve. A lovely spot, this little park leading down to the sea; strange to think that one winter night, more than 20 years ago now, the deadly Clouseaus of the French security services were noisily dragging their inflatable dinghy down the green lawn to begin their amphibious assault on the *Rainbow Warrior*.

That was a boom time all round for Auckland. Architects, whose careers had been governed by decades of tight credit and dirigisme, couldn't believe their luck. To three young architects returning from the UK it must have seemed the right time and place to start a practice. Patrick Clifford, Malcolm Bowes and Michael Thomson, the partners in Architectus, had attended Auckland University's architecture school together, and were simultaneously in London, where Clifford and Bowes worked for an architect who had studied with Louis Kahn. The transmitted knowledge of the great American architect was, and through two decades has remained, an influence on the clearly expressed, built-to-last architecture of Architectus.

Somehow, Architectus survived the '87 crash and the vicissitudes of the following years; the partners'

friendship was undoubtedly crucial to the firm's continuance. For the architectural profession — hardly uniquely — this was a time of Social Darwinist trial. Architectus was pretty fit by the end of the 1990s, heading into the new century having designed two of the most acclaimed buildings of the previous decade: the Clifford-Forsyth House (1995), and the Mathematics, Statistics and Computer Sciences Building at Canterbury University (1998). Since 2000 one strong Architectus building after another has been realised: St Peter's College Technology Block (2001), beside Auckland's Southern Motorway; the West Stand at Christchurch's Jade Stadium (2002, with Athfield Architects); the Population and Health Complex at Auckland University's Tamaki Campus (2005); Henderson Library and the Waitakere City Council Civic Centre (2006) . . . The list goes on: a record of consistently high achievement.

One result of Architectus' success in the field of institutional architecture is its increasingly infrequent acceptance of residential commissions. The practice is not alone in finding it difficult to accommodate domestic architecture within an office set up for larger-scale work. Significantly, the last private residential project that Architectus completed was the Trinity Apartments complex that looks across Parnell Road at the Anglican cathedral (a building that reveals it's a long while since God had the best architects). What may be said about Architectus, though, is that while, at least for the present, it may not be much involved in designing houses, it brings a level of care and attention typical of residential architecture to its bigger-building work.

Previous spread: The north-facing deck off the main floor.

1 family room
2 guest room
3 store
4 terrace
5 bedroom
6 dressing room
7 laundry
8 pond
9 living room
10 kitchen/dining
11 courtyard
12 garage
13 motor court
14 study

LEVEL 4

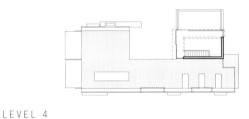

LEVEL 2

LEVEL 3

LEVEL 1

Perhaps the clients who commissioned the Stanley Point House helped prepare Architectus for the practice's move into the public realm. This is not to suggest they sent the architects looking for institutional succour, but this house was a long and complex project. Architecture, one tends to forget, is more slow business than show business. World wars can be launched and lost in the time it takes to design and build a suburban house. The clients at Stanley Point were particular (why shouldn't they be?) and patient. They first approached Architectus in 1997, and the house wasn't substantially finished until 2002. In the years between the design of the Clifford-Forsyth House and the start of this house, the architectural pendulum had swung from post-modernism back towards modernism. This shift, one feels, suited the inclinations of both the architects and the clients of the Stanley Point House just fine.

Parts of the brief for the house read like a modernist manifesto. The clients wanted 'an honest, unadorned building that is refined in its simplicity' and 'shows what it is made of'; the house would have 'a certain reductionism', employ an 'economy of materials and shapes'; and exhibit 'workmanship that pays attention to details without being "precious".' There was a list of instructions specifying the number and nature of the rooms required and, more generally, indicating the house's desired disposition. It should sit firmly on its site, for example, and have sheltered terrace areas and protective eaves; rooms should have daylight from at least two sides; the design should catch and channel the sounds of the sea. There were environmental and performance criteria to meet, some of them not all that common. The architects were briefed to accommodate in their design the clients' concerns about electro-magnetic pollution, for example (all electrical wiring was taken around the perimeter of the house), and 'geopathic stress' (bedrooms were not to be sited above discernible water courses or electro-magnetic fields).

Thomson puts it simply: 'The house is a journey down a sloping site, past a series of open and closed courtyards to the deck.' The 'journey' — a bit of a walk in the park as, besides bordering the public reserve to the west, the house abuts a private estate to the east — ends in a pavilion-like space looking over a lawn and through pohutukawa to the bay. The concrete structure is screened by a cladding of Lawson's cypress; the long, thin strips of timber emphasise the house's horizontality and the sense of procession towards the sea. (Is this a house that wants to be a boat? Or does the north view have a magnetic effect? Perhaps it's all that wiring around the perimeter.)

Inside the house is airy and light but, unlike some contemporary houses built next to the sea, does not require its occupants to wear sunglasses. The material palette is simple — wooden floors with some terrazzo, hoop-pine walls and ceilings, white-washed block walls — and consistent throughout. ('Every room is different,' one of the clients says, 'but the language remains the same.') A lot of thought has gone into this house, and it could have been over-intellectualised, or rather, over-interrogated, but it has emerged as a calm and efficient family home. 'You could take everything out of the house,' one of the clients says, 'and you'd still feel good about being in it.'

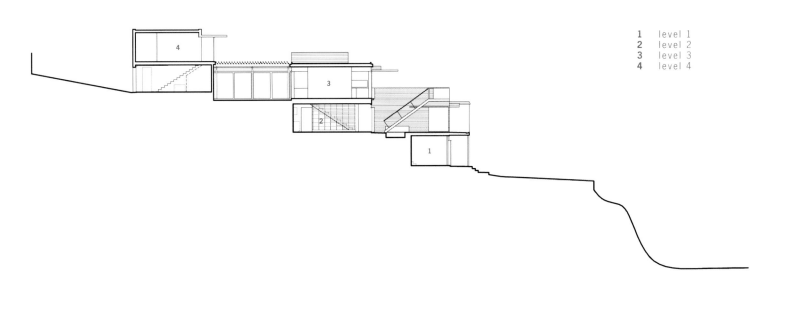

1	level 1
2	level 2
3	level 3
4	level 4

The west elevation faces
and 'borrows' space from a
small park.

Right: Looking up at the house thorough native foliage: the photographer photographed.

Facing page: The layered forms of the west elevation.

Left: Looking to the north, through the kitchen and over the main deck.

Facing page, top: Looking down the spine of the main floor towards the entrance.

Facing page, lower. In the living room, looking across to Bayswater Marina.

The house at dusk, viewed
from the neighbouring reserve.

KAITAWA HOUSE

10

DAVE LAUNDER
ARCHITECT

TE HORO

2004

IN 2007 A NEW Zealand Institute of
Architects jury gave this Dave Launder house
a supreme award, its highest honour, and it's
easy to see why. Here is pure architecture:
a house designed by an architect for himself and his
partner Isobel Gabites, on a site of their choice, in a
place that's not exactly remote but is pretty much out
of sight. More than that, it's a building in which the
typical materials of modern architecture and of New
Zealand rural construction — steel, concrete and wood
— are deployed to withstand the elements without
confronting the landscape. And more than that, it's a
work that is the result of both experience and risk-
taking, an appealing combination to architects, who
must keep hoping, as they get older, that they'll still
get opportunities to take some chances. Jury members
who had been traipsing around inner-city suburbs and
affluent beach settlements must have sat down in this
house, looked out over the crumpled countryside to
the Tasman Sea in the distance, and sighed with relief.

Although the house is, like all buildings, an arrival,
it is strongly expressive of journey. At the most obvious
level, this quality is related to the house's location; as
Dave Launder put it, in a brief but evocative comment
in *Architecture New Zealand* (July/August 2005),
"being there' is influenced by 'getting there". The route
to the house is a topographical tour de force; it goes
inland across the Te Horo plains, passes through a
'tunnel' of totara, crosses a wooden suspension bridge
over the Otaki River, and then heads uphill to a
grassy terrace, an island of flat land bordering a deep
gully, and backed by a mountain range. Movement,

literally, defines this landscape. It is windy and watery
— reminiscent, in its restlessness, of the sea. Perhaps
that's one reason why the house's owners — both of
them sailors — picked this place.

The journey analogy is also suggested by the
shape and placement of the house. Simply, it seems
to go on and on. From end to end it's 40 metres long:
a progression of 4-metre-square modules that are
framed in steel and partially walled-off in pre-cast
concrete. From the east, the marching order goes: a
three-module guest house; a single-module entry; and
six modules or 'pockets' of house proper — kitchen,
dining, living, more living, bed, bath. There is
something primitive or, rather, deeply human, about
the diurnial pursuit of the sun encouraged by the
house's layout and its totally glazed north elevation.
'The rhythms of the day see us migrating linearly
from room to room', Launder has written, 'from one
end of the house through to the far end and back, as if
playing out some ancient cycle . . .' (*Architecture New
Zealand*, July/August 2005). This migration doesn't
quite go to plan; it's only natural that it occurs along
the more open north side of the house, rather than via
the corridor that shoots down the south side.

The sense of being in transit is reinforced by the
positioning of the long, narrow building. In an act of
architectural and engineering bravado, Launder has
stretched the house across a gully which is also a water
course. This is seeking, not just meeting a challenge:
why would an accomplished mountaineer — which,
among other things, Launder is — settle for a familiar
route? The way Launder puts it, the house with its

gull-wing roof is 'the land in section' turned through 90 degrees to face north. So the house becomes a bridge, propped up on steel supports that look as graceful and vulnerable as the legs of a wader bird.

Unsurprisingly, this symmetrical bridge turns out to be not a straightforward thing. It starts out, on the east end, sitting solid; at the west end, though, having traversed the gully it touches the ground very lightly, on just one corner. If this really was a bridge it would seem to have a basic flaw: travellers would be suspended, not delivered. This is a good place to call time on this trope, but even considered in its own terms the house seems to reach an ambivalent conclusion. It's not ended, it's open-ended, and anyone using the bathroom at the transparent western end might well feel that things have been left dangling.

There's no point in designing your own house if you can't make and break the rules. Launder has not followed a straight professional path, and this house is entirely consistent with his history of intrepid pursuits and, perhaps, his inclination to restiveness. Again, the metaphor of journey seems appropriate. Launder was a contemporary of some of New Zealand's more distinguished architects — practitioners such as Gordon Moller and Jon Craig — but when they left architecture school to get cracking on their careers he went off on a climbing expedition to the Patagonian ice-cap. He has practised architecture in New Zealand over many years — he keeps coming back to it — but besides the mountain-climbing there's been the sailing, the time spent as a government architect in New Guinea, the parallel career as an industrial designer . . .

'We don't do flash,' Launder says, speaking for himself and Isobel Gabites (another polymath: biologist, ecologist, designer, writer), and he speaks wistfully of the house's predecessor, a two-room shed that still stands near the edge of the vertiginous ravine. He has cited as an influence William of Ockham, the medieval philosopher who was an enemy of superfluity. The new house has been pared to 'what it needs to be — to be what it is'. But a focus on sufficiency, it turns out, shouldn't be mistaken for justification by function alone. It's not hopelessly frivolous to suggest appearances matter. Thus, the angled sun screens that shade the north elevation, Launder allows, make that face of the house 'prettier' and the deck, which reads as a 'jetty' pushed out from the 'bridge', offers no support to the house but looks like it does. Most dramatically, the south elevation — the arrival side of the house — is clad in sheets of rusting steel, brown as a Jersey cow. Architects love rusting steel, for its texture and its machine-age connotations. A cladding of rusting steel is an application of history.

This is a rigorous house in a vigorous environment. (In winter, there might not be too much migrating from the module with the wood burner.) Launder has likened living in the house to 'working a yacht': 'The rolling doors open and close rooms like sail changes. Louvres are reefed down or spill the breeze when needed.' (*Architecture New Zealand*, July/August 2005.) In other words, life in the Kaitawa House is an architectural adventure.

1   guest bedrooms
2   bathroom
3   laundry
4   landing
5   breezeway
6   deck/patio
7   kitchen
8   entry
9   dining
10 snug
11 living
12 bedroom
13 wardrobe
14 bathroom

Views of the rear or southern
side of the house, with its
rusted steel cladding.

Facing page: North elevation, overlooking the gully.

Above: Looking down the north side of the house, with its serried ranks of modules.

Right: Sitting area, and the corridor that runs down the south side of the house.

Below: Dining and kitchen modules.

The house, straddling the
course of a creek, viewed
from the north-west.

11 ZINCHOUSE

PATTERSON ASSOCIATES

COROMANDEL PENINSULA

2005

IT USED TO BE that one of the more common topics of New Zealand architectural debate was the question of regionalism. Like anything to do with architecture in this country, it was mainly an intramural concern, and like most discussion of local distinctiveness it has come to seem increasingly irrelevant — more dead duck than moot point. Particular sites, as always, present their problems but the solutions can come from anywhere. Put it down to 'globalisation', the triumph of the ubiquitous over the autochthonous. Today, architecture is as rootless and restless as any other pursuit.

But, somewhat paradoxically and rather reassuringly, while architectural production might be deracinated, the producers themselves often seem quite representative of their place. For example, it's almost impossible to imagine Auckland architect Andrew Patterson living in and working from any other New Zealand city. Patterson is a performer. Over the last decade his practice has been responsible for some of the most expressive architecture in Auckland: the D72 building (1997) on Dominion Road, kitted out in basket-woven aluminium cladding; Site 3 (2001) in Newton, a tough composition of concrete buildings and cobbled courtyard; Cumulus (2003) in Parnell, an office building faced in patterned glass reinforced concrete (GRC) that, declares the project's NZIA supreme award citation, displays 'an organic response to materials probably last seen in Auckland in Lippincott's University of Auckland clock tower'.

These are all private-sector buildings — it would be interesting to see Andrew Patterson turned loose on a multivalent public project one day — but because they

are all visible from the street they contribute to the civic realm. They give more to the streetscape than most public buildings, and what they offer, to a citizenry that has come to expect clumsy or offensive architectural manners, is some wit and virtuosity. Patterson's urbanity and his architectural optimism — he's not just a showman, he's certainly a give-it-a-go man — are reminiscent of a type of mid-twentieth century Auckland architect. No; not the guys in The Group, manifesto in one hand, hammer in the other, and a flagon open on the deck, but practitioners like Peter Mark-Brown and Tony Mullan, who somehow made the business of architecture seem as bright and breezy and enjoyable as sailing in the Hauraki Gulf.

In the way of all prospective partners, clients and architects size each other up for compatible fit. Because he is an adventurous architect Patterson attracts adventurous clients (or, at least, people prepared to have a flutter). What's more, he seems to be adept at developing a narrative expression for each architectural quest: a project 'story' that is a compelling apologia for plan and form. Thus, this house at Matarangi on the Coromandel coast, is, Patterson says, 'a representation of history' — the idealised history, that is, of the New Zealand family beach holiday.

The story the home tells is a story of sheds, apparently so simple that it's almost a cartoon history. Four structures make up the compound, an arrangement that alludes to the extemporary development of the Kiwi bach site, traditionally an agglomeration of elements that shacked up casually over the years: a house, then perhaps a sleepout, eventually a boatshed,

maybe an old caravan towed onto the section. Here, Patterson telescopes the evolutionary process. His sheds, though, are sited with care and clad to contrived effect — the thickly corrugated sheets of zinc are punchlines in a broad joke. The Zinc House is a stage wink at history, a caricature portrayal of two types ensconced in New Zealand lore: the shed and the bach.

However, this isn't fun at the expense of function. The house is, intentionally, a simulacrum, but it's an out-of-sight improvement on its models. Patterson's doing a Ralph Lauren, re-presenting a classic vernacular item in designer mode: better made, more comfortable, and far more expensive. Like a new leather jacket that comes scuffed-up and softened, the house is an arrival, reached without a journey, and relies upon an implied narrative to suggest a history where none exists. So the separation of the sheds, Patterson says, might hint at a legacy of long family occupation, perhaps might even give echo to those summer conversations between bach owner and weekend guest that really do occur, elsewhere: 'Grandad built this, and then Dad built that . . .'

The conceit is rather betrayed by the building material chosen to express it. As far as the house's story goes, the zinc cladding is just too good to be true. Patterson notes that, unlike good old corrugated steel which, on a seaside house, would start to rust in a couple of years, the zinc, with its soft, gunmetal patina, 'looks like it did on the day it was built, and always will'. That, presumably, is just fine by the clients; historical allusions are well and good but they naturally want to accumulate their own holiday memories. And Patterson has recognised this. The spatial arrangement of the Zinc House — a courtyard set-up of two-storey boatshed with bedrooms at the rear, single-storey sleepout to one side, and two double storey living/sleeping sheds connected by a pavilion to the front — allows for a harmonious separation of functions and generations. 'Who wants family holidays filled with arguments?' Patterson asks. 'In the old structure of corridors and rooms family peace must have lasted one day.'

Family holidays are not just about escape from each other. While the leeward side of the house offers shelter and a retreat, most of the occupants will spend most of their time, sociably, on the seaward side. The ground floor at the front, apart from the kitchen, is really a verandah; glass doors push back to dissolve the boundary between the pavilion's interior and the deep deck that stretches like a stage along the north-facing front elevation. The house looks to the sea over a wide lawn planted with pine trees, a reserve which is public space but doesn't quite read as such. Some pedestrians come right up to the house for a squiz; others keep their distance — they might suspect they're trespassing.

The pine trees are the making of the development in which the Zinc House is located. Somehow the developer was persuaded to depart from another Kiwi tradition — the instincts of the developer are those of the pioneer: they're clear-fellers, both — and refrain from a chainsaw massacre. Many New Zealand beachfront settlements are sun-blasted heaths, but here the pines provide shade while admitting light, and allow for views without making them available all at once. Pine trees and 'tin' sheds: this is the architectural ego in Arcadia.

1   kitchen
2   dining
3   living
4   deck
5   ramped access
     to beach
6   bathroom
7   bedroom
8   guest room
9   boatshed/
     accomodation

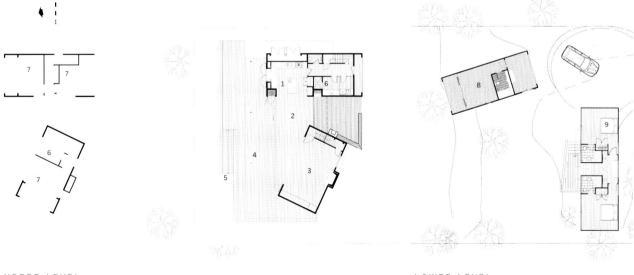

UPPER LEVEL   LOWER LEVEL

Above: View from the sand
dunes showing the pavilion
linking the two double-storeyed
wings of the main structure.

Facing page: East volume,
with a bedroom above and
kitchen below.

ZINCHOUSE

Above and right: Living area, showing the pavilion linking the two main structures fronting the reserve.

Facing page: The guest room, which forms the east side of the compound.

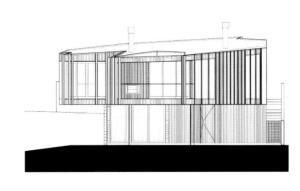

12 ONETANGIBEACHHOUSE

STEVENS LAWSON
ARCHITECTS

WAIHEKE

2007

THE CLIENTS FOR THIS beach house on Waiheke Island live on a south Auckland farm so kempt and well-ordered one wonders whether it hasn't been set up as an advertisement for the dairying way of life. On a knoll at the top of a curved farm road, the family house, too, looks as though it was sited to complete an ideal composition. The house, designed by Terry Hitchcock, an eminent Auckland architect still going strong after 45 years of practice, is as comfortable and sturdy as a worn-in brogue. It's only 13 years old but it looks like it's been there forever — a total contrast to what the house's owners wanted in their new bach on Waiheke. On the island, they wanted something 'edgy'. Hence, Stevens Lawson Architects.

The clients have been holidaying on Waiheke for more than 30 years. When they started going to their old bach — a classic little box still standing alongside the new holiday house — a trip on the Waiheke ferry was as exotic and sometimes as pungent an experience as a bus ride through a Third World hinterland. On the old *Baroona*, bach-owners lugging DIY materials caught up with islanders returning from a visit to New Zealand; pets and poultry were allowed aboard, but the crew tried to draw the line at ruminants. One of the clients recalls a row about a goat which, having been allowed aboard, showed its ingratitude on the gangway as it disembarked. Animal misbehaviour didn't faze people who'd been farming for decades, and nor did roughing it in a basic Waiheke bach. When it came to the design of their new bach, sited at the end of a bay and, therefore, a cynosure of the gaze of everyone reaching the natural

terminus of a stroll along the beach, these clients had no wish to express an ostentatious rejection of traditional island mores. So the new beach house was to be 'recessive' as well as 'edgy'.

The house nestles against the cliff-face on the eastern end of the beach. Actually, nestles is too passive a description, given the assertive process of rock removal and subsequent cliff shoring necessary to make room for the house on its tight site. The house is pushed back into the rock wall, following the line of the cliff to the north, and departing from it at the south end. At the north end the house is obscured by a mature pohutukawa, a 'crucial' element, architect Nicholas Stevens says, of the site, and influential to the plan. (The tree offers shade and a filtered prospect of the beach to the main bedroom, and forms a canopy over the ground-level deck tucked against the cliff on the north side of the house.)

The south elevation is the most sculptural: a plane of slim, vertical, black-stained cedar boards sitting above a wall of unpainted concrete blocks. The best view of this elevation is that available from the bach behind the house; the neighbours no doubt regret the lost sight of a bit of the bay, but, if it's any compensation, they do — when the blind is up on an upstairs slider — get a tantalising framed view through the house to the pohutukawa on the north side. (The owners of the beach house say they are becoming more relaxed with the other side of the viewing deal on a beachfront site; that is, the price of seeing is being sometimes seen.)

The colour of the cedar cladding is, the architects say, consistent with the design's recessional intent. Black

Previous spread: View from the upper bedroom through a pohutukawa tree along Onetangi Beach.

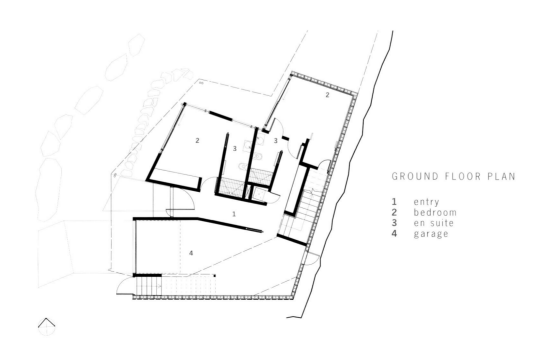

GROUND FLOOR PLAN

1 entry
2 bedroom
3 en suite
4 garage

is the colour of many of Stevens Lawson's recent houses; it is, as they say, resonant in New Zealand, being the colour of sporting nationalism and traditional creosoted baches. More than that, the architects, one suspects, and the clients, just like it. The black stain could have made the house what the clients expressly did not want it to be — a show-off building bossing its context — but it's a dull not a bright black, approaching the colour of burnt driftwood. (The clients' aversion to shiny finishes is also apparent in the matt surfaces of the interior, one slippery-surfaced bathroom unit aside.) The shapes of the house, its clefts and cavities, also militate against the monolithic tendencies of black buildings. Furthermore, the 'fins' that provide, with their variations on irregular patterns, some screening to the upper level blur the outlines of the house, while admitting light. These 'fins' are sufficiently abstract to be infinitely suggestive. Myself, I think they're rather evocative of the palisade of a pa (which must have been a common sight, once, in these parts).

The architects describe the shape of the two-storey house as 'a croissant'. The kitchen is, appropriately enough, at the centre of the concave form on the upper level. In front of the sculptural kitchen island — this is not a house of quadrilaterals — a deep deck faces to the north-west, across to the headland at the far end of the bay, and out to sea. This space is, as the architects say, rather like a stage, but life in this house is not a big production. It's quite an achievement to have designed, and had realised by an able builder, a small house of considerable complexity that functions with intelligent simplicity.

'Everything was done for an ease of life,' says one of the clients; appropriate, she adds a little ruefully, 'for our stage of life'. All the furniture may be used outside; every space that can be used for storage is used — 'we had to grab every square inch'; the television is kept behind a wall of black cedar; the speakers are hidden in the wall. The object was to make the most of the space by keeping it free of too much stuff, to preserve the distinction between the home left temporarily behind and a house to be enjoyed for a few weeks at a time. Comfort and shelter haven't been overlooked: a small rear deck with fireplace, for example, offers a retreat when the north-west wind hits the front of the house.

Simplicity hasn't meant austerity. The materials used on the interior are rich (and they're not cheap, either): terrazzo floor downstairs, oiled American oak floor on the upper level, oak doors, and an oiled cedar ceiling. The ceiling slopes down in one plane; the clients describe it as 'a stingray', while the architects liken it, with its cut-ins and cut-outs, to a tailoring pattern, more Comme des Garçons, one thinks, than Savile Row. This is a surprising house, in many ways, but its owners don't seem surprised at all. They wanted edgy, and at the far end of a beautiful bay, that's what they've got.

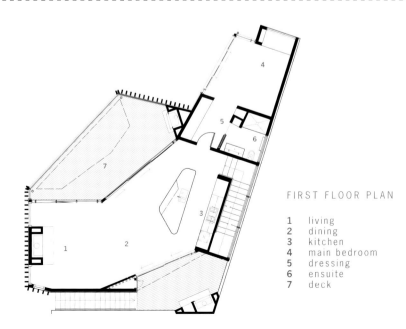

FIRST FLOOR PLAN

1 living
2 dining
3 kitchen
4 main bedroom
5 dressing
6 ensuite
7 deck

Facing page: Screens provide
privacy and shade, while
allowing views out to the beach.

Above and right: Looking from
the balcony on the upper floor.

Facing page, top: Looking to the balcony and kitchen from the living area.

Facing page, lower: The kitchen with rear balcony beyond.

Above: The living room and balcony, beneath the sloping, cedar-clad ceiling. The sculptural cabinet at the south end houses a television above the fireplace.

Left: Main bedroom, with the cliff face beyond.

Above: View of the house
from the beach.

Right: Downpipe and
structural post lashed
together, nautically.

Facing page: Detail
of screens, seen
through pohutukawa.

Above: Looking at the house
from the road, towards the
bush-clad headland at the
eastern end of Onetangi.

Facing page: The house lit up
at night.

BUTLERHOUSE

13

FEARON HAY
ARCHITECTS

WESTMERE,
AUCKLAND

2005

Previous spread: The internal courtyard of the Butler House. Large, retractable, glazed sliding doors allow seamless transition between interiors and courtyards.

IN CERTAIN PERIODS, CERTAIN practitioners of an art or craft are so attuned to the tenor of their time it seems they've been chosen as the official channel of the zeitgeist. Ratings are high, one could say, and funding seems assured (though care must be taken that repeats don't weaken the brand). Jeff Fearon and Tim Hay, both of them not long out of architecture school, launched their Auckland practice at a propitious moment (1998), not that they were to know it then.

The economy was soon to begin the process of recovery from a decade of socio-fiscal experimentation, and in architecture postmodernism, a meretricious style just right for a gauche and grasping era, had run its local course. At the fin de siècle, and with the end of the millennium nigh, where to next? Back to the future. Modernism, with its discipline and its renunciations, was once more rather alluring. (The approach to a new millennium seems to encourage repentance.) With less seeming like more, it was natural that architects would again have Mies on their minds. Plan B? Plano. The Farnsworth House (1951) in Illinois provided many of the ingredients for the new Kiwi Pav(ilion).

Fearon Hay Architects hit the ground running, quickly winning awards and publicity for projects such as the Rawhiti House (1999) and Coromandel Beach House (1999). These early commissions were, in significant part, pavilions on beaches. Nothing particularly novel in that; what was different, though, was that a form of International Style was, after all these years, being realised to international standards. Aside from design competence — a given, though not

to be taken lightly — what continues to characterise Fearon Hay's houses is the quality of their materials and the sophistication of their detailing and finishing. The houses are polished by money.

Quickly successful and almost immediately celebrated, Fearon Hay inevitably became a lightning rod for criticism of the sort of architecture — spare but seductive, restrained but rich — with which they are identified. 'Magazine architecture' is the epithet that's often tossed around; it means that a building, not coincidentally, looks 'good' in photographs, or is flattered by the camera. (Could it just be that the building simply can be more readily comprehended in photographs? Perish the thought.) Malcolm Walker, the Auckland architect who is also the cartoonist for *Architecture New Zealand*, has had some fun with 'magazine architecture'. 'Doing a house in the 21st century — it's so easy', declared the caption of one of his cartoons (see page 15). 'Draw a long thin box . . . No, longer and thinner is better. Elevation? Same as for plan. Add windows for photographic effect. Jam onto site. Jam in owners. Jam in magazines.' (*Architecture New Zealand*, May/June 2002.)

Blaming Fearon Hay for the spread of a photogenic, neo-modernist orthodoxy is hardly fair. For one thing, they're not responsible for the performance of second-rate fellow-travellers; for another, even their critics allow that they're very good at what they do. (Inside 10 years, the practice has racked up eight NZIA New Zealand awards for architecture and a supreme award.) A practice, especially one still young, that caters to a wealthy clientele, is bound to attract social democratic

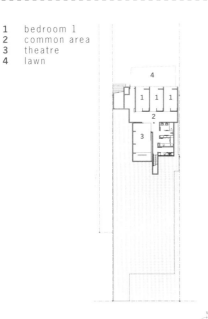

1 bedroom 1
2 common area
3 theatre
4 lawn

BASEMENT

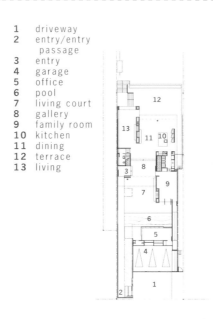

1 driveway
2 entry/entry passage
3 entry
4 garage
5 office
6 pool
7 living court
8 gallery
9 family room
10 kitchen
11 dining
12 terrace
13 living

GROUND

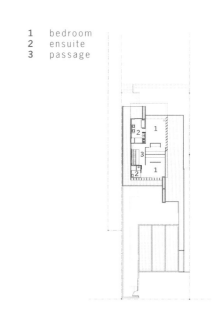

1 bedroom
2 ensuite
3 passage

FIRST

cavilling but there remains a suspicion that Fearon Hay's houses are just too glamorous. When they discuss Fearon Hay's work, architects of a certain age probably know they're going to sound like grumpy old geezers, but they can't help themselves. How can people take possession of such self-possessed buildings? Who's in charge — the inhabitants, or the houses? (Well, by now Fearon Hay's clients do know what they're getting.) Behind the visceral reaction, there is, perhaps, an intellectual resentment about the fate of modernism. Over a couple of generations, modernism has repeated itself, first as brutal programme (think the 1960s tower blocks of British cities), then as mere form. Modernism the movement has become minimalism the style.

It can't be denied that Fearon Hay have an impressive way with space, or rather, with the enclosure and framing of space. The Butler House is arranged to take full command of its clifftop site in Westmere. Like a couple of Pete Bossley houses a few doors along, and unlike Stevens Lawson's Cox's Bay House (see pages 274–287) further down the road, the Butler House gives the street the cold shoulder. The rejection is pretty definitive, and reads as a particular riposte to the cantilevered overture of the house across the street; the neighbour's jutting frontage hangs there like a proffered handshake. In front of the garage doors a cobbled strip planted with grass — a kind of angry lawn — seems to mock the traditional suburban verge.

Screened on three sides, and open only to its sea-side on the west, the house is really a world of its own. Mostly, it's a platform for living — a pavilion. The cars are out of the way, and so are the kids' rooms, down on the ground floor level. A courtyard with pool is at the centre of the site; there's a continuous spatial flow through to the living areas, and then to the terrace overlooking the Waitemata. The glazed elevation at first floor level seems to stretch to take in as much as possible of the three horizontal elements of a wonderful view: Meola Reef, Birkenhead Point and, farthest away, the Waitakere Ranges.

The clients wanted a house that would 'have the look of permanence' and that's what they got. It's hard, and in places, it's heavy. Floor surfaces are limestone tiles and wood; the walls are plastered; solid doors swing on pivots; and two concrete benches are deployed, massively, Jeff Fearon says, 'to anchor space'. (The client says it took 20 people to carry the kitchen bench into the house.) For all the expensive fittings and clever technology in this house — this is a motorised building, a panzer compared to the average foot-slogging bungalow — its real luxury is space. Fearon talks of 'spaces moulded by the architecture', and of a sense that the various spaces in the house have been 'carved and hollowed out'. Especially in the living areas, it could pass for a highly refined cave; its depth offers welcome relief from the bright coastal light.

This is a large and tough house, a fair-sized challenge to a youthful practice (Fearon Hay began the project in 2000). A challenge, too, perhaps, to the owners. They like their house, but there's a lot of it. You wonder, when encountering Big Minimalism, whether lifestyles expand, carp-like, to fill the available space. Thinking of your own goldfish bowl, you might also wonder: wouldn't it be nice to have the chance to find out?

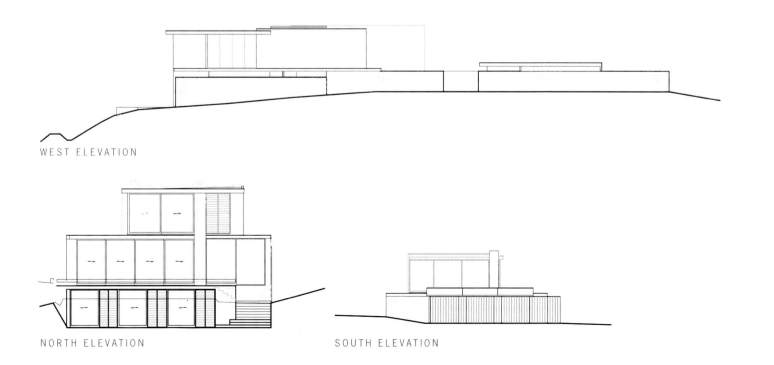

WEST ELEVATION

NORTH ELEVATION

SOUTH ELEVATION

Above: Looking over the palm-clad walkway into the internal courtyard.

Right: Street elevation.

Facing page: Inner courtyard, with pool.

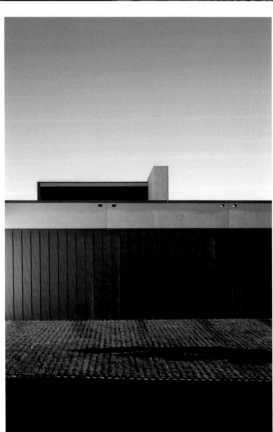

Looking from the inner
courtyard through the house
to the sea.

Above: The living and dining
areas are separated by a
massive wall containing
fireplaces facing into
both rooms.

Facing page, top: The only
circular element in the whole
building: the column that runs
from top to bottom through
all three floors.

Facing page, lower: The living
room is oriented to catch the
afternoon sun.

The corridor between the
garage and the main house.

Above: Top of the landing.

Left: The solid kitchen bench.

175

PAROA BAY HOUSE

14

PETE BOSSLEY
ARCHITECTS

BAY OF ISLANDS

2003

Previous spread: The main
house with its hyperbolic
parabaloid roof.

THE BAY OF ISLANDS is where it all started for New Zealand, as modern nation and political entity. Kororareka, a shanty town of ruffians and renegades not much given to bothering God, was our first entrepôt. Sure, the business and religious promoters of colonisation quickly seized the opportunities presented by Britain's imperial reach, but the eventual success of their project doesn't alter the fact that New Zealand began on the beach. (Mentally, we're still there.) The early years of culture contact in the Bay of Islands provide New Zealand history with some of its more colourful elements and its most significant moment: the signing of the Treaty of Waitangi. Climatically benign, physically beautiful, the Bay of Islands is where the taming of Aotearoa got underway.

So, more than 150 years on, how's the civilising mission going? Pretty nicely, to judge by this house, sited on a sheltered valley floor, right above a beach in a bay not far from Russell. Busby, Hobson, Fitzroy — those early imperial agents whose careers ran aground in the Bay of Islands — could never have imagined the district would furnish such evidence of order and prosperity. (The architecture would have been beyond them, too.) The whole mise en scène might have occurred to the Reverend Samuel Marsden, but only as a vision reconciling divine providence and human industriousness, and even then the notion of a holiday house would have been incomprehensible to a Low Church mind.

The past is unusually present in the Bay of Islands, and it's hard to avoid historical references. It cannot be a coincidence that it's in this part of New Zealand, more than any other, that Pete Bossley has explored the concept of the holiday house as encampment. This has always been a region of beach camps — for centuries Maori made seasonal migrations to the coast, and the tradition of the summer settlement received cross-cultural expression in the camping grounds of the twentieth century. In a series of Bay of Islands houses, dating back to the Heatley Houses (commenced in 1999), and including the Paroa Bay House and projects about to be realised, Bossley has separated the components of large dwellings, pushing them progressively further apart. Like a young beach cricketer instructing fielders, the architect seems to be saying 'back, back, back . . .'

Bossley is working with large sites on these projects — the Paroa Bay House sits at the edge of a 20 hectare estate, half bush, half grazed — and has long since arrived at the liberating conclusion that there is no need, in such contexts, to bunch everything up. The challenge is to find the right balance between separation and unity. (The fielders, one might say, should not be stationed so remotely as to be effectively out of the game.) There's a term for this state of spatial equilibrium: it's a courtyard, and that's what Bossley calls the area between main house and outhouses in his 'campground' projects. It is a little bit of a stretch — that centre, can it hold? — and as such is typical of the work of an architect who has always been prepared to acknowledge the tenuousness of architecture's control. (Hasn't everything, right from the start, been flying apart?) Bossley's buildings are so expressive of

1 living
2 kitchen
3 covered terrace
4 office
5 laundry
6 main bedroom
7 bedroom
8 sitting area

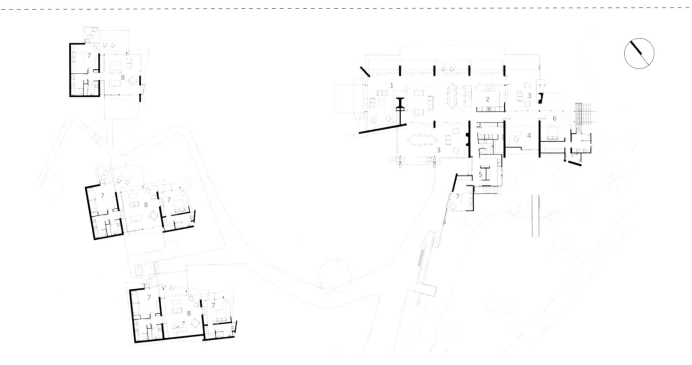

their making that they seem also to countenance their deconstruction. They're suggestive, because while Bossley explores ideas he does not reach doctrinaire conclusions. He does have a lot of ideas, and admits this profusion needs supervision. 'Buildings shouldn't be over-laden with ideas,' he says. 'Each one should have its own voice.'

While Bossley is not interested in promoting a style, he says there are 'underlying approaches that run from project to project'; ideas, convictions really, about light, mass, space and comfort. The latter is 'almost a dirty word in architecture', and coming after Bossley's talk about ideas it is a bit surprising to hear him say it. But he is well aware of the difference between experimenting with forms and testing clients' tolerance. A house is not an adventure playground: 'Dynamic spaces don't make rooms.' OK, Bossley is responsible — and at the upper end of residential architecture a lot is at stake — but he doesn't want to bore anyone, least of all himself. He likes to mix things up: 'I don't have a moral compunction about materials,' he says. 'I don't believe one is more appropriate than another.' His disposition to juxtaposition finds pretty full expression at the Paroa Bay House, a composition of counterpoints: togetherness and apartness, heaviness and lightness, solidity and transparency, and, most basic of all, building and landscape.

The main house in a complex of five buildings — there are also three guest houses and a boat and implement shed — is an apparently contradictory form: a grunty pavilion. Like its sibling structures it has a steel frame, concrete walls and concrete floors, overlaid with stone pavers. A thousand cubic metres of concrete went into this project, and 60 tonnes of reinforcing steel. If that seems to defy local construction tradition — surely this is lightweight land? — a visit to Russell will reveal a venerable precedent: Pompallier, with its rammed earth walls, built as a printery by the French Marists in 1842. The full length of the pavilion — its essential 'pavilion-ness' — is only apparent on the elevation that faces the sea. From the bay the house is the upper of three striated forms; it stretches low along the ridge of a lawn which runs down to a sloping retaining wall above the sand. At either end the house is bookmarked by a mature pohutukawa. (There's a thesis topic here: The role of pohutukawa in the beach architecture of northern New Zealand.)

The house sits on its apron of paved terrace, whereas the guesthouses are dug into the side of a hill. Grass is planted on the roofs of these outbuildings. One wears its lawn cut in a number two; the others are topped with tufts of tall grass, like hair implants on the head of a bald man. The guesthouses are well-appointed, of course, but cannot have the graceful horizontality of the seaside elevation of the main house. The interior of that house is a calm and generous space, naturally warm even on a winter's day; it gives out onto a sheltered terrace on the lee side. Light is brought in from above, as well as from the sides, via a clerestory beneath the house's singular architectural gesture: the hyperbolic parabaloid roof above the main living area. No exaggeration, the roof's like a sail. Or perhaps the fly of a tent. Or maybe a wave. Something ephemeral, anyway, to offset all that monumentality below.

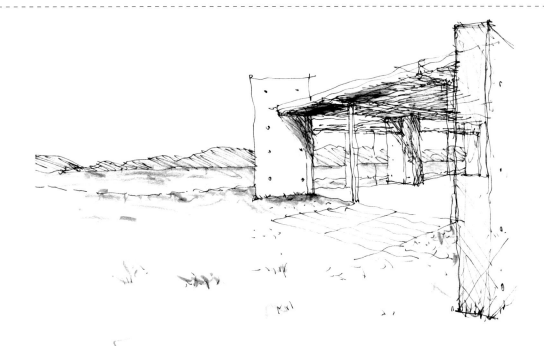

Facing page: Looking down on
the main house and its outliers
and out to Paroa Bay.

Above: On the front terrace.

Facing page: Looking across the lawn to the rear terrace of the main house.

Above left: Main living area, under the parabaloid roof.

Above: Looking along the front of the main house from the kitchen.

Left: In the sitting room, looking back to the kitchen.

Seaward elevation.

Left: The main house, at dusk.

Below: The front of the house
is framed by pohutukawa.

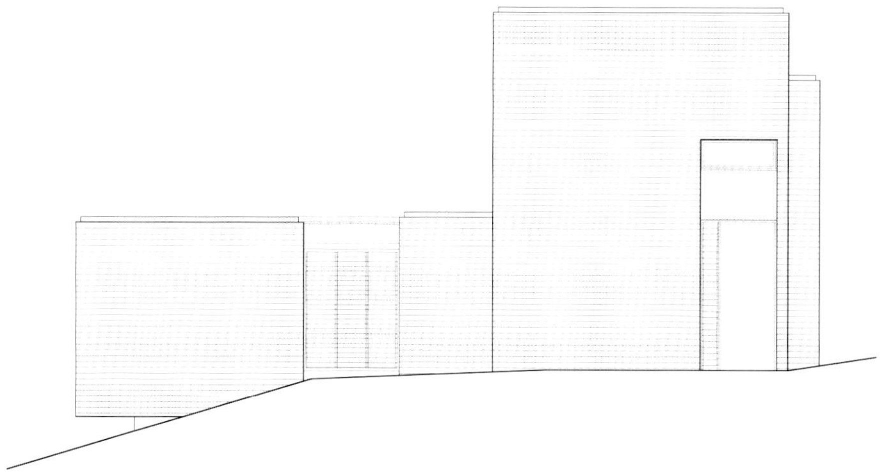

HUGHES–KINUGAWA HOUSE

15

ANDREW LISTER
ARCHITECT

WATERVIEW,
AUCKLAND

2001

ARCHITECTURE IS A BROAD church — the spectrum of practice ranges from the pragmatic to the poetic. Many architects are conventional professional men (architecture in New Zealand is still a gendered profession); meeting them, one does think that there, but for the grace of a graphic gift, goes a lawyer or accountant or engineer. Others, however, seem more right-brained: their buildings, particularly their houses, read as works of art. Consequently, those buildings receive a complex reception, especially from their designers' peers. Appreciation is undercut by envy of talent and opportunity, expressed in purse-lipped censure of 'object' architecture.

What is the problem? If a house looks 'good' — an admittedly subjective judgment, but one that can be formed after rational consideration of factors such as relationship to site, clarity of composition, and grace of proportion — and if it works for the clients who paid for it, then surely it is exemplary architecture. That a house may evidence some self-conscious awareness of appearance is not necessarily proof of meretricious intent; street-appeal is not just the province of the street-walker. Well, at least not in those societies where the populace has long been disposed to strut its stuff; New Zealand, suburban and protestant, has never gone in for the passagiato.

Over the past decade Andrew Lister has designed a series of small, artful houses around Auckland. Although the houses are each quite different in their form — 'I don't have a signature style,' Lister says — they have in common a sculptural quality. 'I try not

to make my houses look like houses,' he says. 'At least, not like traditional houses.' The Hughes-Kinugawa House was the first house Lister designed after starting his own practice. It's at the end of a street — the best saved for last — in Waterview, an unpretentious suburb in Auckland's inner west in which, needless to say, most houses do not have water views. This house sure does, though, and more. Perched on a steep, west-facing site, it overlooks a shallow tidal reach of the Waitemata Harbour. The sea comes and goes under a bridge in the motorway a kilometre to the north, washing through mangroves on either side of a narrow channel. It is a very Auckland environment: estuarine, not too kempt, and squint-makingly bright in the afternoon sun.

While the house seems to sit as lightly on its site, it is in fact tethered firmly to it. More than that, the foundation and retaining work entailed in construction holds the land together: the ground beneath the subdivided section was an unstable platform of road-building rubble. Lister's client Owen Hughes says he has ended up with what is effectively a pole house — 'not that you'd know it,' he adds, as even the biggest wooden piles, 12 metres long, are buried from view. The fragility of the site had obvious material implications — concrete, for example, was not a flooring option — and, in general, the house is a response to restrictions. The art pursued here is the art of the possible.

From the street, the house is two walls of wood. It is a sculptural perspective, contrived, Lister says, to reveal 'no hint of a door or window'. The visible elevations are the east and north sides of the larger of the two connected boxes that form the house. It is a

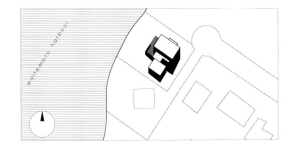

Previous spread: The double-height living area faces west across a tidal reach of the Waitemata.
Below: West elevation.

small house, less than 120 square metres, including the deck — 'the size of a Ponsonby worker's cottage,' says Hughes — and small houses with modest budgets are not easy. 'You sweat blood on these projects,' Lister says. Moreover, on this job the architect had to swallow a double-dose of design prescription. Besides the usual council regulations, the height-to-boundary and set-back provisions that influence, if not govern, site and shape, Lister had to comply with unfamiliar client requirements. Hughes' wife, Yuri Kinugawa, wanted the house to conform to the principles of 'direct compass', a Japanese spatial philosophy that is apparently analogous to feng shui. This requirement, it's fair to say, did lead to some designer, and spousal, head-scratching.

In the course of the project, Lister produced three designs. The first, a sloping form that Hughes likens to 'a wedge of cheese', was scuppered by a height-to-boundary complaint, and the second — 'two strong cubes' — fell foul of a 'direct compass' ruling. The third iteration passed bi-cultural muster. Although 'direct compass', with its precepts on boundaries and proportions, is an arcane system, Hughes says it seems to produce 'common sense' design solutions. In this case, the built result of the meeting of occidental planning law and oriental design philosophy is a house that rises to the height limits, provides some surprisingly generous volumes, and achieves functional separation between public (living) and private (sleeping and bathing) areas.

The Hughes-Kinugawa House, says Lister, 'is shaped as much like a Japanese jewellery box as I could make it.' Though tight, it isn't mean. Lister has scrimped and saved enough space to allow for a splurge in the living area. The 'public' box is divided into a two-storey back, with two bedrooms/offices, each with a clever horizontal balustrade-cum-shelf, and a single-volume front. A floor-to-ceiling run of bookshelves emphasises the verticality of this front room; the top shelves can only be reached by a sliding ladder — it's as though a slim section of a reading room from an Edwardian public library has been smuggled into the house. In terms of spatial economics, this void should be read as investment, rather than expenditure; it's the means whereby a small inside leverages off a big outside.

The smaller box, cantilevered to the south, is, with its tatami sleeping platform and bamboo ceiling, more overtly Japanese. This one-room box performs a single task; in contrast, the structure between the 'public' and 'private' boxes has quite a bit to do. As well as providing a short connecting corridor, it accommodates the bathroom and separate toilet. The house here does seem crimped, probably for reasons beyond the architect's control. On modest projects such as this choices are often binary in their simplicity — it's either/or design. So, for example, the choice of wood cladding over glazing on the east and north elevations is a vote for street wall over morning warmth. But the clients like their house, and they enjoyed the process of its design and construction. The house is a lesson — an object lesson — in design efficiency, and it raises an increasingly relevant question: how much space do we really need?

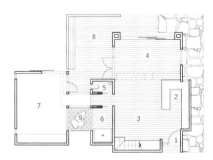

GROUND LEVEL PLAN

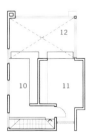

UPPER LEVEL PLAN

1   entry
2   kitchen
3   dining
4   living
5   wc
6   bathing
7   main bedroom
8   deck
9   courtyard garden
10   office/bed
11   bedroom
12   void

Facing page: Looking along the west elevation.

Below: The solid forms of the street elevation.

Above: Bathroom.

Top right: Bedroom.

Above right: The kitchen fits under the upper-level bedroom.

Right: Looking from the kitchen through the double-height living area.

Facing page: The double-height library wall on the north side of the house. Shelves are accessed by a sliding ladder; the wall is pierced by a T-shaped window.

HOUSE

HALL

16

PAUL CLARKE
CROSSON CLARKE
CARNACHAN ARCHITECTS

WANAKA

2004

ONE OF THE MORE notable
phenomena of recent New Zealand history
has been the renaissance of Central Otago.
Apart from the 1970s campaign to prevent
the damming of the Clutha River to build the Clyde
Dam, the region hasn't received as much attention
since the discovery of gold laid the foundations for
southern fortunes 150 years ago. For most of last
century 'Central' was a picturesque backwater, kind of
known about, reputedly special, but hardly a celebrity
district. What was its pen portrait in school geography
lessons? Stone fruit, sheep stations, skiing, and the
steamboat on Lake Wakatipu. Some may also have
heard about, or experienced, the children's health camp
at Roxburgh, one of half a dozen such facilities set
up around New Zealand between the wars to beef up
'malnutrits'. The camps were supported by the sale of
postage stamps depicting happy children at outdoor
play, attended by smiling nurses: a pastoral idyll, with
social welfare — just what New Zealand used to think
life here was.

All reveries have to end. In the 1990s Central
Otago got its wake-up call, or rather, wakey-wakey!
call. Adventure tourism, property development, the
wine industry — they all came knocking. And in
the train of money: architecture. It's true, the region
was not, previously, entirely bereft of architecture:
architects had designed holiday homes in Wanaka
and Queenstown, and some civic buildings, and a few
large hotels. But what was obvious about the built
environment — such as it was, in Central Otago
— was that its virtues were vernacular. Utilitarian

buildings, with schist walls and tin roofs, were the
characteristic structures of the region. There probably
isn't an architect anywhere who doesn't love this
simple type, and the urge to invoke it is as strong in
the south as the compulsion to reference the 'bach' is
in the north.

Needless to say, it's an urge that often has
regrettable consequences. Whereas the materials used
in traditional Central Otago buildings, especially
the local stone used for exterior walls, were integral
to construction, in new buildings they're often just
decorative. There's nothing wrong with a bit of make-
up, but it can't compensate for clumsy proportion or
ungainly posture.

A couple of other general points may be made
about architecture in Central Otago. First, the
region's old buildings were designed to protect
and enclose — that, in a remote district with New
Zealand's most extreme climate, was quite enough
to be getting on with. Second, those buildings were
intended for permanent, or at least regular, occupation
or use. Contrast these properties with those of the
new architecture of Central Otago, most of which
is domestic. Protection is no longer dependent on
enclosure: money and technology have made the solid
wall an option, not a requirement. As for duration of
habitation: at the architect end of architecture many, if
not most, of the region's houses are homes to be used
for holidays or in retirement. Time being limited, it is
of the essence; if you're not going to be in a place for
long, you might want to grab as much of it as possible,
as quickly as possible. And what is the most valuable

local commodity? The view. Again, it wasn't always so; Central's residents used to be more concerned with the weather; for them, the view would always be there — they didn't have to gobble it up.

So, now, anything is technically possible. You want a pavilion on a few exposed hectares near Wanaka? Well, may we offer for inspiration — to paraphrase Paul Clarke's account of an early client meeting on the Hall House — Philip Johnson's Glass House, at New Canaan, Connecticut (1949), and Mies van der Rohe's Farnsworth House, at Plano, Illinois (1951). No pressure, then. On the other hand, may as well get it out there — every architect asked for a glass pavilion must immediately think of these two exemplars. (For transparent buildings, they sure have cast a long shadow over the last half-century of Western architecture.) After Mies and Johnson, then, the Hall House: a rectilinear box with a minimally pitched roof, floated above the ground on a concrete slab, with floor-to-ceiling windows offering 270-degree mountain views. Not after Mies and Johnson: an accompanying wooden box with garaging and self-contained one-bedroom accommodation, and a third compositional element: steel mesh gabions filled with Cardrona River stones.

This house is what it is, and where it is, because of the landscape. A glass pavilion, of course, is an essay in boundary dissolution; it's the next best thing to being in a landscape. As Clarke says, with a house such as this, the landscape becomes artwork: what you have on the walls when you have no walls. But, wait: though this house is transparent, it has not disappeared. It

is itself an object in the landscape. Clarke says he wasn't overawed by the landscape, although it would be totally understandable if an architect were to be humbled by the topography of Central Otago, the part of a crumpled skinny country that most resembles a continent. However, he has felt the need to respond. Some of his design decisions are the smart answers one would expect from a good architect to particular questions posed by the site. For example, the house is positioned in a natural gully, lessening its exposure to the nor'wester and thereby, Clarke says, making it two or three degrees warmer.

Other aspects of the design, though, suggest that a landscape as powerful as the one that surrounds this house can exert a gravitational pull that would take Miesian discipline to resist. So, for example, the gabions offer privacy and filter sunlight but, with their caches of local stones, they are also indigenising gestures; sculpture, perhaps, as placatory offering to place. Then there's the ground shaping by landscape architect Megan Wraight — a series of small weirs, and lined-up rows of tussock — that mediates some of the space between the house and the big beyond. Engagement with the landscape, or a matter of not leaving well enough alone? Perhaps it's just that, in a sublime landscape, lonely objects need a bit of company.

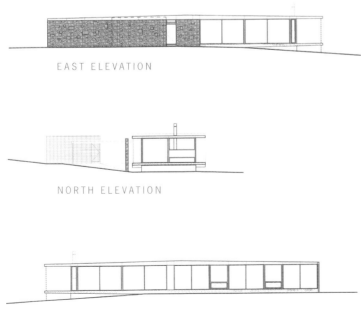

EAST ELEVATION

NORTH ELEVATION

WEST ELEVATION

Above: The north end of the
pavilion, looking west.

Left: Looking into the kitchen
and main living area.

The house is cantilevered
above the ground at its
north end.

FLOOR PLAN

1   living
2   dining
3   kitchen
4   entry
5   bedroom
6   bathroom
7   ensuite
8   laundry
9   garage

The site is ringed by snow-capped mountains.

The gabion wall between the
main house and the garage.

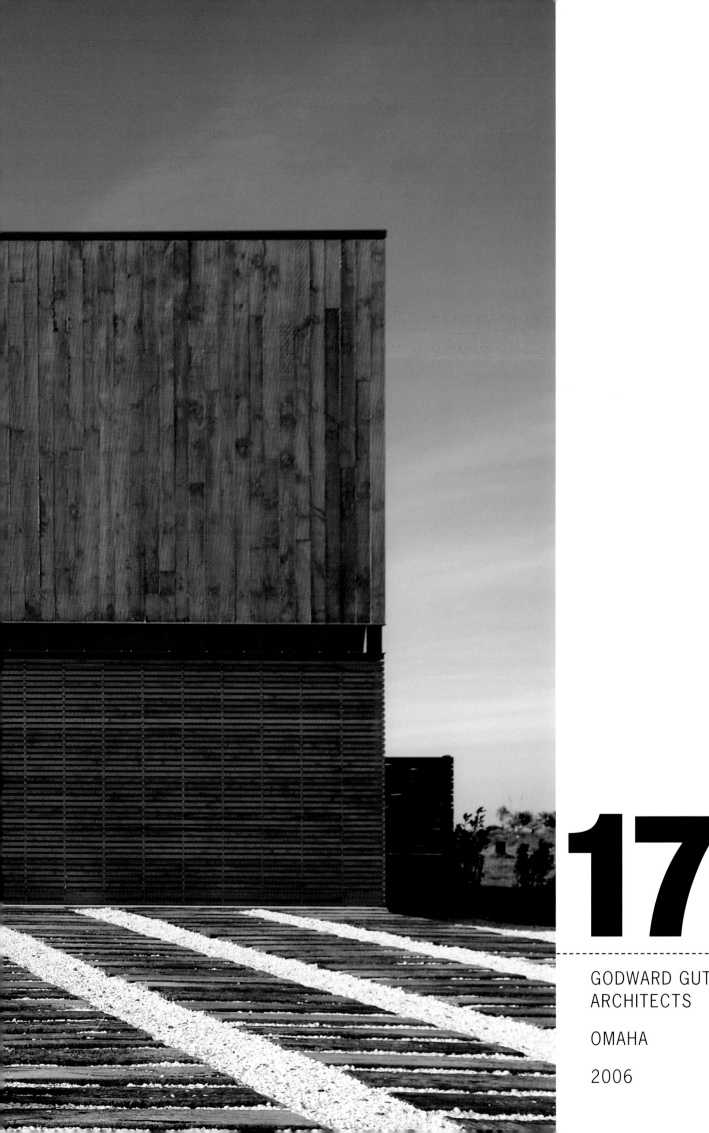

17 CROSSHOUSE

GODWARD GUTHRIE
ARCHITECTS

OMAHA

2006

ON A COLD WINTER'S day architect Julian Guthrie and I stand at the threshold of this house, vainly trying to open the front door with an ill-cut key. 'There's your story,' Guthrie says. '"Writer finds Omaha beach house as impenetrable as the neighbours do".' Perhaps, but he's certainly correct that the house gives little away. It's not that the house is inscrutable; rather, it's rejectionist. It communicates a disinterest in the surrounding built environment that, inevitably, will be read as disdain. The message the house imparts is that if there is any architectural conversation occurring at Omaha, it's not one worth joining. Best just to get on and do your own thing.

The uncompromising form of the house raises a philosophical question: can one be neighbourly when there is no neighbourhood? Omaha is a beach development on a spit of former farmland, reached by a causeway, an hour north of Auckland. Holiday houses started going up there several decades ago, but the Omaha subdivision on which the Cross House sits is a recent, and more upmarket phenomenon. It is a hybrid place: not really a suburb or even a settlement, more a coincidence of buildings. Omaha, one begins to think, could have been designed to illustrate the point made so memorably by Margaret Thatcher: there is no such thing as society, only individuals and their families (and their beach houses?).

The non-communal nature of Omaha is indicated by the absence of social facilities — there are no shops, cafes, bars, schools or churches (although there are a couple of public tennis courts) — and the disposition of houses. Many, seemingly, are just plonked on their

sections and then contorted to grab a bit of sea view. 'Object' architecture may not be the goal of such self-interested 'architectural' behaviour, but it is the result. A viewer is encouraged to look at Omaha's houses as discrete objects because there is not much else to look at on this flat and windy littoral. The lack of vegetation is not explained merely by the weather and the newness of construction. It's also related, Guthrie says, to the regulations and covenants governing the placement of houses on their sites. In order to provide view lines through the development, houses must be set back two metres from their boundaries; to preserve these visual corridors planting is restricted. Flora in Omaha runs the gamut from grass to shrub.

Covenants and planning diktats are notoriously incapable of guaranteeing good architecture. Especially away from the most expensive beachfront precincts, Omaha is a mad geometry lesson of acute-angled roofs, pop-up upper levels and cantilevered boxes. (Oh for a good old single-storey wooden pre-fab.) It is against these prevailing standards of design that the Cross House presents its stern and unforgiving face. The snub starts at the street. Instead of an orthodox concrete drive through a strip of lawn the house is reached by rows of railway sleepers set in a screed of white shells. The house, on this public side, is tough, mute, almost industrial. Factory-made, concrete panel walls clearly expressing vertical formwork are counterpoised with movable, horizontally slatted wooden screens. When the screens and the slim aluminium shutters on the garage wall are closed no openings are visible on this facade — no door, no windows, no way in.

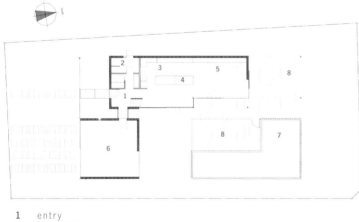

1   entry
2   bathroom
3   kitchen
4   dining
5   living
6   garage
7   pool
8   deck

GROUND FLOOR PLAN

1   study
2   master bedroom
3   bedroom 2
4   bedroom 3
5   bathroom

FIRST FLOOR PLAN

1   deck

ROOF PLAN

The stern approach is maintained along the sides of the two double-storey cubes that give the house its compact form. Only at the rear, around an L-shaped pool, does the house open out. Although protection and privacy were imperatives that drove the design, the point of being at the beach is to be able to see it, and building to the 7-metre height limit has allowed for the incorporation of what is effectively a third level: a roof top 'room' that offers 360-degree views over its enclosing parapet.

While the exterior of the house is raw and monolithic — because the concrete panels are pre- and not in situ-cast they don't require sealer joints — the inside is smoother in its finishes and relaxed in its planning. As soon as visitors come in the front door — but not before — they can relax. Entry leads immediately into the living areas or up two flights of stairs to the main bedroom and then to the roof exterior. Materials are simple — fairface concrete walls, Tasmanian oak floors, seagrass matting on the upper floor — and internal volumes are big. At night, Guthrie says, the house lights up like a lantern.

The brief for this house, the architect notes, is 'quite suburban' — three bedrooms, a two-car garage — but he adds, 'I wouldn't have designed it for a suburban street.' Well, in many suburban streets, the architect may not have been allowed to design this house. The Cross House, Guthrie says, is 'a good coastal response' in its form and composition. In other words, it responds to the wider site and to the elements; what it does not acknowledge is the neighbourhood. Realistically, if sadly, there was no alternative. The Cross House is a rebuke to much of the building at Omaha and might, therefore, occasion some pique. Because the houses around it are no match for it, the house comes across as a bit of a bully, quite taken with its own tough looks. Like a boxer in an easy division, what the Cross House needs is some tough competition.

In contrast to the solid outer walls, the structure on the courtyard side is slender and the house is open.

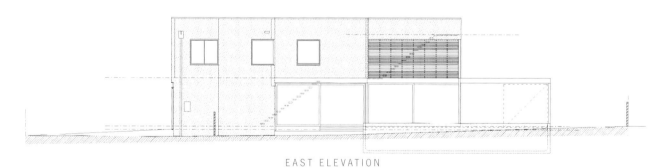

EAST ELEVATION

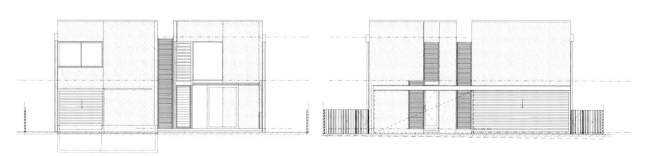

NORTH ELEVATION   SOUTH ELEVATION

Above: Looking down from the roof terrace onto the pool area.

Right: Looking across the pool to the garage wing. The two volumes are connected by glazed walkways on both floors, sheltered by timber screens.

Far right: Pedestrian approach to front entrance.

Facing page: On the north terrace stacked, sliding, glazed doors allow the main living area to be opened to the courtyard.

Above: The living room and
kitchen, with the entry beyond.

Right: The dining table is an
extension of the kitchen bench.

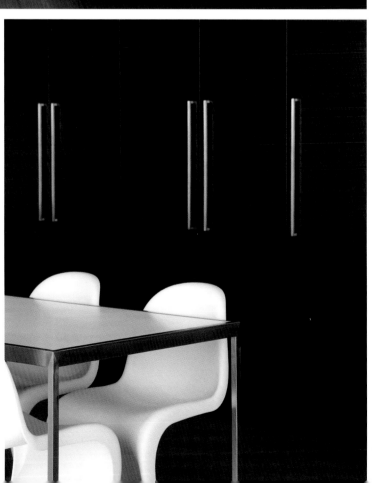

The double-height volume of
the sitting room.

Kitchen, with stairs to the
upper level in the foreground,.

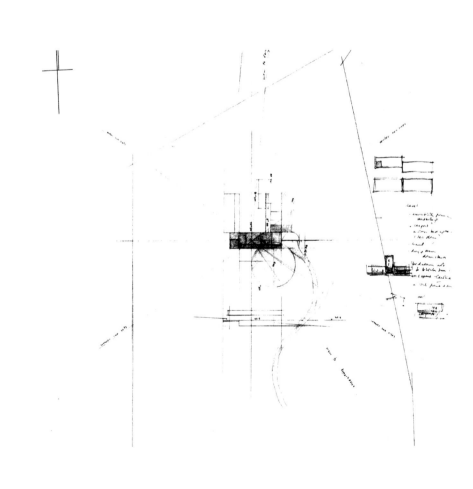

VANASCHHOUSE

18

FELICITY WALLACE
ARCHITECTS

QUEENSTOWN

2003

RESIDENTIAL ARCHITECTURE, in its pure form — that is, an architect designing a house for clients who will actually live in it — is normally an intense business. The architect is spending a substantial portion of the clients' savings and future income and is, literally, giving shape to much of their lives. And, as the cliché goes, substance to their dreams (we'll return to the psychoanalytic dimension of architecture later). Moreover, architect and clients will be part of each other's lives for several years. Many marriages are over in the time it takes to design and build a house; come to think of it, many marriages are over because of the time it takes to design and build a house. The potential for changes of mind — whether induced by budget blowouts, interfering friends, or a recent edition of an Italian design magazine — is limitless, as is the scope for discussions about fittings and fixtures. Little wonder that one of New Zealand's more distinguished practitioners has confessed that 'every architect gets to the stage where if they have to have another conversation about taps they'll scream'. (Chris Kelly, interviewed in *Houses NZ*, 3, 2007.)

Given that residential architecture is so labour intensive, one wonders whether women are more suited to the genre. Aren't women meant to be more intuitive and empathetic, more skilled at multi-tasking, more attentive to detail? Well, in New Zealand women are probably more likely to pursue careers in domestic design, but that might just be because the old and not-so-old boys who control the large architectural practices are unable or unwilling to reconcile opportunities for female professional advancement with the demands of motherhood. However, in spite of any alleged gender-dependent characteristics that might be advantageous in residential architecture, and in spite of the structural detouring of women into that field, there are few female architects in the top rank of local house designers. Which raises a couple of questions: are the leading male residential architects in close touch with their feminine side? Or, is there something about domestic architecture that encourages the survival of the traditional figure of the hero-architect in his various guises: beau idéal, confidant, boss, Dad?

There is something. As architect Felicity Wallace notes, most of the decisions on most residential projects are made by the distaff side of the commissioning team: women, that is, call the shots, and they maintain the relationship with the architect. Wallace is astute, and demonstrably determined. She is at the forefront of her profession *and* has a large family *and* runs her practice from the small Rangitikei town of Marton, rather a different scene from that of her previous base, above a café in Auckland's High Street. For almost 20 years she has run her own practice, following early-career jobs with Bossley Cheshire and Lane Priest ('Architecture was a lot of fun in the '80s,' she says), a stint in London, and positions, on her return, with commercial practices where, she says, she learnt a lot about high-rise design, the art of costing and the craft of fit-outs. Bored with that, she started out on her own in 1989; the same day she gave notice she met an acquaintance in a café and got her first job. One job led to another, through the lean 1990s, a time of karmic correction after the architectural excesses that accompanied Rogernomics.

1 entrance
2 garage
3 wine cellar
4 drying room
5 office
6 courtyard

BASEMENT PLAN

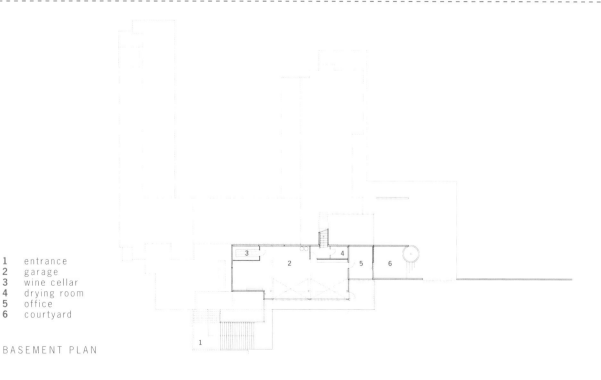

Wallace won the commission for the van Asch House against the competition of at least one other noted architect. The site is a block of land down a dead-end road in a sheltered valley outside Queenstown; it looks north to Coronet Peak and east to The Remarkables (such a Kiwi name for such grandeur; now we'd probably christen the range The Awesomes). The clients, it seems, are rather remarkable, too: opinionated and informed, and possessed, unusually, of both wealth and a strong aesthetic sensibility. 'I can't work with clients who just say, "I like that" or "I want that",' Wallace says. 'If a client has no ideas, then I can't have any, either.' (Now, no male architect would ever have the gumption to make such a frank admission.) In the case of these clients, many of the ideas related to the relationship between interior and exterior spaces and to materiality, expressed somewhat industrially in pre-cast concrete and steel, as well as timber. The female client, Wallace says, wanted a home (was she the advocate of spatial relationships?) whereas the male client tended towards a structure (was he the champion of the hard stuff?). Both, though, wanted 'a permanent home'.

One point of reference was a celebrated house by a famous architect: Richard Neutra's Kaufmann House, in Palm Springs, California (1946). By quoting this work did the clients signal that they expected a close relationship with their architect? The Austrian-American Neutra (1892-1970), a native of Vienna, Sigmund Freud's city, developed very close bonds with his clients; indeed, he seemed to imagine himself as their psychoanalyst. 'I am liked by . . . all my clients,' Neutra wrote. 'It is almost like a love affair that ends happily in,

by far, most cases.' (Cited in Sylvia Lavin, *Form Follows Libido*, 2004.) Of course, this is not at all to suggest the clients for the van Asch House regarded the process of designing and building a house as a psychotherapeutic exercise (although, as a Freudian might point out, why *did* they refer to the Kaufmann House? Shall we analyse that?) No: it's just that a house of this scale is emotionally as well as intellectually demanding. Wallace spent a lot of time on site, latterly with a new-born baby in tow, 'thinking about spaces and levels'. Tired of the 'perfection' of pavilions, she off-set the house's steel frames. 'I kind of deformed [the house],' she says. 'There's nothing that quite lines up.' That's better: out with Freud, in with Kant: 'Out of the crooked timber of humanity, no straight thing was ever made.'

Wallace says her experience of the site told her that, factoring in wind, sun and snow, 'it was simply not sensible to do a flat roof'. Access to the sun is very important in Central Otago, she says: when the sun's out, you need to be in it. 'You also need scale,' she says, 'and you need height to get scale.' Things changed during this project: the original scheme, for example, had the bedroom wing to the west, not the east, of the main wing. The bedroom wing was also originally two storeys, reduced to a single storey to go to tender. One principle that remained constant is that while the house in its form and materials should respond to its site — specifically and broadly defined — the interior should provide comfort, warmth and intimacy. Does that sound like the home from whence we all came, and to whence we all want to return? Oh, get behind me, Sigmund. No, I didn't mean it like that . . .

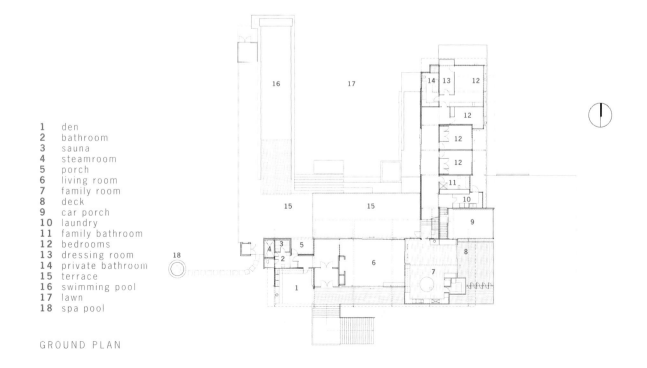

1 den
2 bathroom
3 sauna
4 steamroom
5 porch
6 living room
7 family room
8 deck
9 car porch
10 laundry
11 family bathroom
12 bedrooms
13 dressing room
14 private bathroom
15 terrace
16 swimming pool
17 lawn
18 spa pool

GROUND PLAN

Far left: The van Asch House is in a basin surrounded by mountains.

Above: Looking at the main bedroom, with courtyard to the right.

Left: Looking from the courtyard to the bedroom wing.

Above: The kitchen, with its circular island (right), has views out to the mountains.

Far right: Stair detail.

Facing page: Dining area.

The house has garaging
and an office on the ground
floor, with an east-facing
deck above.

CARNACHANHOUSE

19

SIMON CARNACHAN
CROSSON CLARKE
CARNACHAN ARCHITECTS

PARNELL,
AUCKLAND

2003

Previous spread: Looking from
the garden at the rear of the
house into the double-height
living area.

THIS LITTLE HOUSE IN a Parnell cul-de-sac sits with its face to the past and its back to the future. From the street it presents, over its creeper-covered wall and aluminium gates, sufficient of its original cottage shape and enough suggestive detail to comply with Auckland City Council's heritage requirements. At the rear, to the north-west, it's a modern concrete and glass box giving out to a sheltered courtyard garden. In a way, the house is an act of legerdemain, or even a trompe l'œil: the council and, presumably, the neighbours, get to see what they want to see; the clients — architect Simon Carnachan and his wife, Robyn — get to live the way they want to live.

The house was — and, residually, is — a worker's cottage that, Carnachan believes, dates from the 1860s. When it was built, it would have been on the edge of the harbour. In the early, pre-reclamation years of Auckland's settlement, St George's Bay came to the bottom of what is now a reserve adjacent to the Carnachan House. The cottage might have been a modest structure, but the sloping section it occupied was relatively generous. Constructed before Parnell's streets were surveyed, the house straddled two titles.

When the Carnachans bought the house it was 'a wreck', but in the estimation of the council it was estimable, and its condition did not justify its destruction. The street that the cottage is in is a mini-precinct of heirloom domestic architecture; it's the sort of Victorian and Edwardian residential streetscape the council wants to protect. Heritage regimes can be arbitrary — diagonally opposite the Carnachan House,

in a different planning zone although only metres away, is a new four-storey apartment building — but one can appreciate the desire to preserve some evidence that Auckland has a history.

Just as one can understand architects' impatience with regimes that cramp their style. In 'character' suburbs — usually inner-city neighbourhoods once favoured by the working class but now coveted by middle-class professionals who know their rights and are quick to legally assert them — the arguments over new building are familiar. On the one side, a defence of coherence and continuity which could be interpreted as an assertion of communal values, if only it wasn't also motivated by a concern for property values. On the other, a promotion of innovation and change that can be read as an expression of selfish individualism, but often rises from the basic recognition that we don't live as Victorians did and we don't use our houses as they did.

It's not easy to resolve this conflict and, inevitably, official attempts to legislate for 'character' frequently lead to responses which observe the letter of the law but not its spirit. Because the bigger picture is complex, and because planners and architects see things differently, the debate over the design of a new house in a 'historic' area often narrows to a myopic focus on details and emblematic features. For example, in the case of the Carnachan House, a picket fence, proposed by the council and successfully resisted by the architect.

Simon Carnachan is a very experienced architect. After launching his career with the noted Auckland

1 garage
2 main bedroom/
   bathroom
3 bedroom
4 bathroom
5 void
6 kitchen
7 dining/living
8 library
9 verandah

UPPER LEVEL

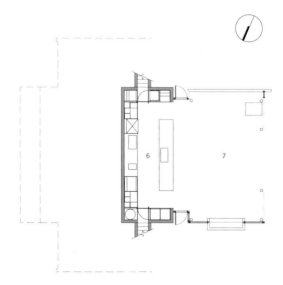

LOWER LEVEL

practice, Mark-Brown, Fairhead and Sang, soon to be Fairhead, Sang and Carnachan, he worked with Ron Sang on two of the most significant local residential projects of the 1970s, the Sargent House (1973) and the Brake House (1976), and he has gone on to design dozens of houses in the city and far further afield. He knows which parameters are set (height-to-boundary ratios, for example) and which are more discretionary or even whimsical (cladding materials, window treatments, fence types). In other words, he knows how to play the game, although he is increasingly frustrated at having to leap through the hoops.

The front of the Carnachan House could be interpreted as facadism, an exercise in face-saving, one could say. Actually, the street elevation is literally a face: a front door with windows on either side, garages at either end as ears, and even a tongue of concrete slab poking out from verandah to gate. The simple symmetry of a cottage continues inside, where a short hall is flanked by a bedroom and bathroom. There's a transitional area used for sleeping and reading — an arrangment that might be disconcerting if the house were not essentially a pied à terre — and then the cottage becomes something else: a two-storey volume of space, walled with tilt-slab concrete and glass shaded with louvres that, Carnachan surmises, the council may have chosen to read as weatherboards. Standing on a glass-floored, vertiginous balcony, visitors might feel they're about to be pitched into the twenty-first century.

What the Carnachans have got is what they wanted: 'a comfortable town house'. The process, says Simon Carnachan, may not have been logical, but it has led to a highly disciplined result. A 'scruffy old cottage' with a 'hideous lean-to' has been transformed, although not beyond recognition. For all intents and purposes, the Carnachans have a new house and, what do you know, although an old house has been gutted the council is not. In fact, says Carnachan, the house now stars in an Auckland City Council video as a model residential redevelopment.

Looking down the hall to the front door, on the upper level.

SOUTH ELEVATION

EAST ELEVATION

WEST ELEVATION

Facing page: View from
the south showing the new
addition to the nineteenth-
century cottage.

Above: Kitchen, on the
lower level.

Right: A skylight marks the junction of the two forms.

Lower right: Looking from the bathroom to the bedroom towards the street.

Facing page: Main living area, with the garden beyond.

Facing page: Void over the
lower level, with the library
at right. The sliding, glazed
screens and glass floor allow
light into the lower level.

Below: Street elevation.

20 COROMANDEL

COROMANDELBACH

KEN CROSSON
CROSSON CLARKE
CARNACHAN ARCHITECTS

COROMANDEL PENINSULA

2002

HERE'S WHAT LOOKS LIKE an open and
shut case: a wooden box, with drawbridge
decks and shuttered windows, on a manuka-
covered hillside above a white-sand beach. It
seems to be a Kiwi bach; in fact, it could be *the* Kiwi
bach. Not merely simple and sufficient, the Coromandel
Bach is reductive and essentialist — the realisation of an
ideal form. It's more than neo-modernist; it's practically
neo-Platonist. The bach may not be Ken Crosson's
defining building — he is a mid-career architect in a
successful Auckland practice — but it is a definitive
project. It reads like the work of someone with a point
to prove, or rather, a thesis to demonstrate; it would be
quite understandable if the architect had hammered
home the last nail with the satisfied flourish of a
mathematician signing off the solution to a nice little
problem: QED. The thought even occurs that Crosson's
self-contained bach might be a means of achieving
closure. The modern bach? He's done it. Can we all, to
use the modern platitude, just move on?

Ownership of a bach on the Coromandel Peninsula
must be one of the stock items of New Zealand
daydreams, giving, as it does, a pleasantly particular
focus to the national fixation with holidays, beaches, and
residential real estate. For most of us, at this juncture in
our history, making bach dreams come true is about as
likely as winning Lotto, but Crosson was in a position
to engage in some actualisation. He and his wife
explored the eastern side of the Coromandel looking for
a suitable site for a holiday house. They found what they
wanted at a bay north of Whitianga, a place with several
situational advantages: it faces north (not that common

a coastal orientation in a skinny country that runs down,
not across the globe); it is relatively remote; and it is
reached by a stretch of unsealed road. (A gravel surface
is still an effective deterrent against development.) Oh,
and the bay is beautiful — a curve of beach mirroring
an arc of islands.

The steep site the Crossons found had already been
prepared for construction. A level building platform
had been scoured from the slope, and a driveway had
been bulldozed up through the scrub. Negotiating a
gravel road, and then climbing through a thicket of
manuka as close as a tunnel: now that's an approach
to a Kiwi bach. The previous owners had intended to
build to the rear of the flat part of the lot — a cautious
ambition that might have imparted a sense of security,
at the cost of distancing the house from its dramatic
environment. Crosson, however, chose not to retreat
before the possibilities of the site, and opted to build
at the front edge of the platform. This strategy still
provides some summer shelter in the lee of the house.

There is nothing special about most of the holiday
houses along New Zealand's coastline. As befits the
architecture of an informal people, these buildings
usually fail to rise to the occasion. Crosson did think
hard about the sort of 'bach' he would design on his
piece of the Coromandel. He belongs to what is perhaps
the first generation of European New Zealanders to
have a clear and relaxed sense of national identity. One
of Crosson's contemporaries, Wellington architect Chris
Kelly, says it wasn't until he read historian James Belich's
Making Peoples (1996) that he realised 'how New
Zealand has only just started to become itself in our

lifetimes' (*Houses NZ*, 3, 2007). It's only natural, then, that Crosson should want to respond to a prototypically New Zealand place with a resolutely New Zealand building. More than that, he says, he wanted something 'regional', and something 'gutsy, not twee'.

Here we go, one is inclined to think. More talk about sheds and barns. But Crosson says he was inspired by other structures: the wooden 'trip' dams built by the loggers who sawed their way through the Coromandel's indigenous forests in the nineteenth century. When he discusses his bach Crosson refers to photographs of the dams, which were crudely effective means of getting logs out of the bush, sending them down water races to rivers or coasts. And the elevations of the bach do bear a familial resemblance to the walls of the dams: both present a simple grid of vertical supports and horizontal boards. The bach's weathered Lawson's cypress cladding strengthens the likeness. On the outside, the bach is as softly grey as the beams of a trip dam in an old monochrome photo.

The bach is a bit of a mollusc: lead-coloured on the outside, all gold inside, the contrast becoming greater as the exterior fades with age. But there's no false advertising here; simplicity is what the bach promises, and simplicity is what it delivers. The programme expresses a basic social organisation: in the middle, a communal area that is an abbreviation of the standard procession of the big contemporary pavilion (kitchen, dining, living); and at either end a ply-walled bedroom pod, one (with the larger bathroom) for the parents, and one (with the smaller bathroom) for the children. The kids get bunks; perhaps when they're older they'll

fight for the rights to the spare bedroom. The laundry is hidden behind sliding doors, and several cupboard spaces provide storage.

Refreshingly, this family seems to regard a bach holiday as an opportunity to do without stuff, rather than acquire more gear. The careful approach to the apportionment of space is relieved by a few liberal gestures: the swinging chair hanging from the ceiling in the living area, the architect's drawing board in the main bedroom, the wheeled bath that may be pushed out on to the deck.

Although the bach's fireplace suggests winter occupation, this is really a summer house; it is more tent than cave. Despite its picture-perfect oceanic site and regional references, the Crossons' bach has quite a lot in common with the season-specific holiday houses of the northern hemisphere, the mountain cabins or beach houses that are the sites of the annual rituals of arrival and departure, opening up and closing down. Typically, New Zealand 'baches' or holiday houses don't work like this; on the coasts, especially, they must earn their keep all year round. The hint of seasonal specialisation tests one's faith in the Coromandel Bach's proclaimed 'bachiness'; the presence of such clarity and order disrupts it altogether. Crosson hasn't really continued a tradition; he has realised, quite exquisitely, an idea. This building is resonant, all right, but it's more than a gesture of typological homage. Rather than being seen as a bach it could, perhaps, be read as a container or a packing case, deposited by a freak wave on a lonely shore. A coda, in other words, for the settlement of this place.

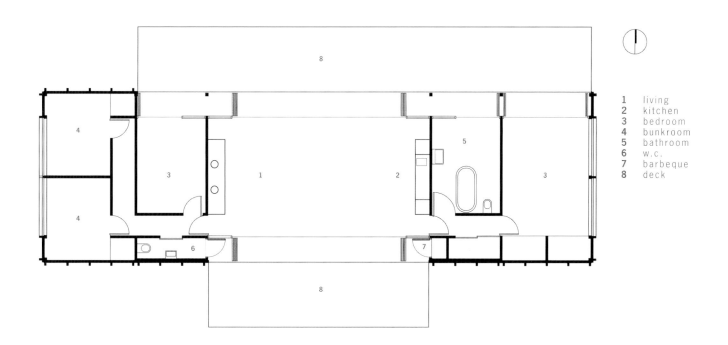

1 living
2 kitchen
3 bedroom
4 bunkroom
5 bathroom
6 w.c.
7 barbeque
8 deck

Above: The bath can be rolled outside on its castors.

Right: The bach in shut-down mode, with the decks on the north and south sides raised to secure the building.

Above: The bach with decks
lowered. Behind the kitchen
is the bathroom and main
bedroom.

Facing page, top: The
fireplace occupies the end of
the main living space, opposite
the kitchen.

Facing page, lower left:
Looking into the bathroom
from the deck.

Facing page, lower right:
Dining area and kitchen.

Above: The bach from the flat
lawn to the south.

Right: Looking out from the
living area to the front deck,
and to the Mercury Islands.

WALKER HOUSE

21

MITCHELL & STOUT
ARCHITECTS

COROMANDEL
PENINSULA

2005

Previous spread: The
courtyard, with main living
wing to the left, children's
and guest accommodation
to the right, and plunge pool
in the foreground.

AUCKLAND, HARDLY THE MOST urban of
cities, is perennially deficient in urbane figures.
However, if you're lucky you may catch sight
of one in the CBD, striding off to another
encounter with council bureaucrats or corporate bean-
counters, panama-hatted against the sun and, maybe,
the spirit of these times: David Mitchell, partner, with
Julie Stout, in Mitchell and Stout Architects, and
holder of a New Zealand Institute of Architects' Gold
Medal for career achievement. Mitchell, despite a long
sojourn out of New Zealand in the 1990s (a good time
to be gone), has designed some of the most significant
Auckland buildings of the last generation — public
buildings such as the University of Auckland Music
School (with Jack Manning, 1980) and Auckland Art
Gallery's New Gallery (1995); and houses such as the
Gibbs House, Judges Bay (1983) and his and Julie
Stout's own house in Freemans Bay (1990).

The Mitchell-Stout House is, with Patrick
Clifford's own house in Meadowbank (1995), the most
accomplished small Auckland house to have come out
of the 1990s. Like Clifford's house, it is highly crafted
but quite relaxed; it feels at ease with itself, and at home
in its city. It's an exemplar — yes, one thinks, this is
how houses in this temperate, Pacific city should be
— and, in its excellence, it's a reproach.

Architects in New Zealand generally keep their
heads down — small society, shallow pool of would-be
clients, a media which seems to have a lingering pioneer
disdain for professional qualifications and competence,
etcetera — but Mitchell, and Julie Stout, have stood up
to be counted on public issues. They were outspoken,

for example, in their opposition to the proposed rugby
stadium on Auckland's waterfront. Mitchell is also one
of the few architects to have contributed to the small
corpus of local architectural criticism. His book, *The
Elegant Shed* (Oxford University Press, 1984), remains
influential, and not just because it's practically peerless.
Mitchell writes well, and perceptively.

However, one wonders if the clever title of his
book isn't just too damn resonant. It's not Mitchell's
fault, but the shed — especially the elegant one — is
a trope that has provided cover for designers naked
of ideas ever since the book was published. Does that
book title also engender some cognitive dissonance
about Mitchell's own architecture? Not about its nature
— although if Mitchell's buildings are vernacular they
are so in the sense that All Blacks' rugby is: so advanced
a form of a popular pursuit that it might as well be
another game — but rather about its availability. These
days, a fair degree of affluence is a prerequisite to the
commissioning of a Mitchell and Stout house. That is
not meant pejoratively: the bespoke creations of one of
New Zealand's best architecture practices cannot come
cheap, and Mitchell certainly has paid his dues, teaching
and designing public housing and public projects, many
of them unrealised. (People will one day wonder: why
didn't they just give him some of those jobs and let him
get on with it?) The language of Mitchell's discourse
— even though his style is lapidary, not laconic — does
not trumpet the sophistication of his work.

There's ample evidence of Mitchell and Stout's
mastery in the Walker House. The house is on the
same strip of foreshore as Andrew Patterson's Zinc

GROUND FLOOR PLAN

1 living
2 dining
3 kitchen
4 laundry
5 bathroom 1
6 lounge
7 gallery
8 garage
9 bathroom 2
10 guest bedroom

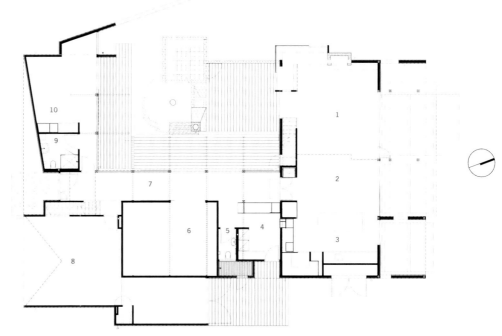

House (see pages 138–149) and several other architect-designed houses. Unusually, the houses in this architects' row are set well back from the beach, a positioning that endows them with what Mitchell calls 'a pleasant golf-coursey front' (complete, however, with spectators). The other natural advantage these houses enjoy is their situation among stands of pines — 'the least loved of New Zealand trees', as Mitchell notes, a condition derived from their commodity status and, perhaps, their exotic origins. They're popular here, though; filtering light and framing views, their presence brings a Nordic home-in-the-woods quality to houses that definitely are not cabins. Without the pines, this area might actually resemble a golf course development, albeit with superior architecture.

Mitchell says his clients were clear about what they wanted: 'a comfortable life on the beach'. That meant making the spatial arrangements and allocations common to beach houses in this architectural band. 'Organisationally,' Mitchell says, the house is 'as obvious as hell.' (Perhaps, but of course the devil is in the details.) Parental quarters are separated from the children's and guests' bedrooms; living, cooking, and dining areas occupy one big, terrazzo-floored space looking out to the beach; the large garage is sited at the rear or approach side of the house. The large screening room is hardly a standard item, nor is the courtyard at the heart of the plan. Visitors look into the courtyard as they go along the hall from the entrance to the front of the house; the guest bedroom opens onto it, and so does the living area, via a big sliding door.

While the clients' aspirations may have been unexceptional, Mitchell says they 'liked the idea of innovation — they wanted something distinctive'. Hence the vertical cedar weatherboard sheathing, a cladding system turned back to front, with the battens on the inside and boards on the outside, held in place by brass washers (and friction). The milled cedar boards reach up in concert with the pines; the brass fixings provide surface decoration for the flat planes of wood.

There are many clever and artful elements in this house. On the outside: the way the house angles in on the ground floor on the south elevation to provide a sheltered entry and sense of arrival; the wooden wall that departs from the house on the west side to form a fourth wall for the courtyard; the deep overhang on the north side, and the narrow rectangular void beneath it, which offers glimpses of the pines beyond; a small, sheltered section of terrace to the front, not totally enclosed, of course. (Framed views, previews, almost — partial, teasing, surprising — are typical of Mitchell and Stout's architecture.) On the inside: the window-seat in the living room, sitting in a box cantilevered off the west side; the void in the wall beside the seat, and the little embrasure in the wall beside the stair leading to the upper-level bedrooms (more peep shows); and the concrete fireplace, expressing its rough, horizontal formwork. Courtyards are favourite Mitchell and Stout spaces, but this courtyard is perhaps over-burdened (or over-briefed). A lot is going on there: changes of levels, a kind of pergola, a pine tree, barbecue area, chimney and plunge pool. It's the only place where the house seems to shed its elegance.

FIRST FLOOR PLAN

1 bedroom
2 ensuite
3 study
4 void
5 bathroom

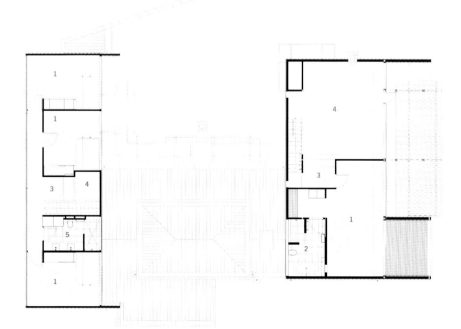

Above: Seaward elevation.

Above right: Rear and side elevations, showing the wall to west that extends to protect the courtyard.

Facing page: The cantilevered window-seat connects the living area to the courtyard and gathers western light.

The house from the lawn to
the front. At present, the site
to the west is empty.

Left: Lounge, showing the lightweight timber structure.

Below: Looking along the central hall towards the front, with the courtyard on the left.

Western elevation, with the
sheltered courtyard in the
middle of the house, beach
to the left, and arrival to
the right.

WALKERHOUSE

22 PARSONSONBEACHHOUSE

GERALD PARSONSON
ARCHITECTS

PARAPARAUMU,
KAPITI COAST

2000

PARAPARAUMU IS ONLY 50 kilometres
north of Wellington, although generations of
children sitting in the back of cars crawling
along the two-lane 'highway' to the 'Gold Coast'
have wondered if they'd ever get there. You didn't
have to be a bored kid to think that 'there' was not a
term that could easily be applied to Paraparaumu, or
'Paraparam', as it was known in linguistically lazier
times. Paraparaumu was never just a bach settlement
—it was the site of the capital's first airport, and
because its climate is comparatively benign, it has long
been favoured as a retirement spot for Wellingtonians
awaiting final departure — but it had the straggly
informality of a holiday place. Now, it's kind-of-a-town,
sort-of-a-suburb, sprawled over the flat land between
the highway and the sea. Architecturally, it is not
distinguished; design ambition — not often justified by
talent — is realised on sites nearest the beach, a long
strip of white sand exposed to onshore winds and the
point-of-it-all view of Kapiti Island.

With his family, Wellington architect Gerald
Parsonson had bought a beach-front section occupied
by an old house 'which slowly fell apart'. It was a
relatively long site — although less narrow after the
family bought the section to one side — and when he
came to design a new holiday house Parsonson sought
to use that length to maximise the separation between
garaging and dwelling. The local council wouldn't allow
him to push garages to the street — perhaps that's
understandable, even though a couple of plain garages
would only enhance most Paraparaumu streetscapes
— but Parsonson has managed to get the buildings

that hide the cars well away from the shelters that
house the people. This strategy puts a little distance
between the experiences of getting to and being at
the beach. Passengers revert to the more natural state
of pedestrians, who are led into the house along a
duckboard pathway — a short walk that effects a
transition from street and suburbia to beach and holiday.

'I spent a long time putting a scheme together,'
Parsonson says. 'I'd been looking at a Calatrava-type
roof, gentle and delicate'. But his wife rejected the
initial design as 'too architectural, too try-hard', and
asked 'for something more basic'. That, says Parsonson,
was the 'right call to make'. A back-to-basics approach
meant looking at what should be embraced (the dunes,
the Tasman and Kapiti), looking away from what
should be rejected (the suburban hinterland), and
acknowledging cultural and material precedent (the
bach). It did not mean a reprise of the 'standard model'
at Paraparaumu Beach: a two-level building with
bedrooms on the bottom, living areas on top, staring
over the dunes but disconnected from its site, and
'packed with suburban stuff'.

What Parsonson has pursued is 'a play between
solid and light'. In its formal composition, the house is
a marriage of bach and pavilion — a human analogue
might be a farmer who has wooed a debutante.
The house presents its plain back to public view, an
orientation that doesn't come across as unfriendly
because it doesn't seem contrived: it's what beachfront
baches have always done. On this, its rear or arrival
side, the house, with its panels of green, fibre-
cement cladding, looks familiar. Unlike many of the

1   boardwalk
2   entry
3   kitchen
4   dining
5   living
6   deck
7   laundry
8   wc
9   bathroom
10 bedroom
11 guest
12 carport

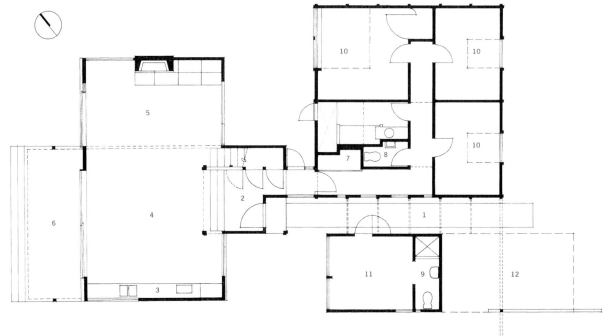

contemporary holiday houses allegedly related to a bach, the Parsonson beach house actually resembles one.

There, is, though, a lot more to the house than first meets the eye. The house is a collection of structures: a bach-like box for the family's bedrooms and another for guest accommodation, and the living pavilion on the sea-side, lifted off the ground — but not too much — to gain views across the lawn to the ocean and Kapiti Island. There's also a tower, raised above the clever entry module — part vestibule, part airlock — which efficiently handles the arrival of the wooden walkway, the departure of the parallel corridor running back to the bedroom block, the change of level to the living areas, and the lift off to the observation room.

The house is a careful assemblage that only gradually draws attention to the art of its devising. (Not too 'architectural', then, but definitely architecture.) Although built in one go, the house suggests the accretive nature of bach construction. 'It has an ad hoc feel to it,' Parsonson says. 'People have asked, "What part did you build first?" You can't read it all at once — the longer you stay, the more things you see.' Parsonson has had some fun with the house's design (if the back is all about history, the front is all about geography), materials (fibre-cement cladding and black-stained weatherboards) and details (tiny shuttered windows and self-designed furniture), but the humour is always in good taste. There is nothing — especially, and most unusually, not a television set — to detract from the central experiences the house offers: graceful ease in the pavilion, with its floating roof, and comforting simplicity in the bach, with its basic bedrooms.

Parsonson is right: the house is a clear expression of the relationship between solid (and shelter) and light (and exposure). The house's interior colours emphasise these functional differences. Pale colours are fine in the sunny 'pavilion' but, Parsonson says, if used in the 'bach' the bedrooms 'would die'. Instead, the semi-detached bedroom wing is a red and green block, reached via a red hallway — a colourful trip to the cave. The architect was reading about Paul Klee when he was designing the house; another colour prompt came from the memory of a favourite among a childhood collection of shells, one that was bright orange on the inside. This house, so connected to its site and so free of the material clutter of suburbia, should be a locus of happy memories for the architect's family. At Paraparaumu Gerald Parsonson has achieved something rare: a holiday house that is both relaxed and resolved.

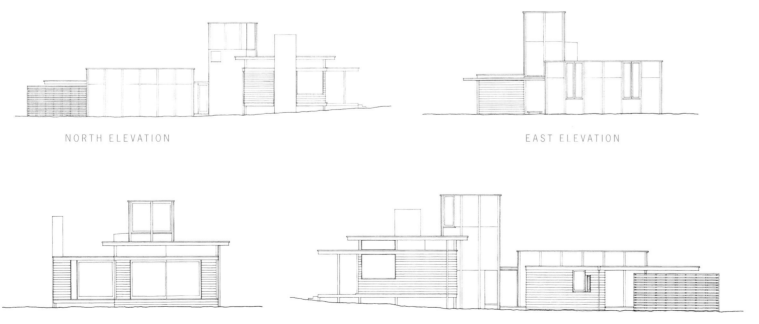

NORTH ELEVATION

EAST ELEVATION

WEST ELEVATION

SOUTH ELEVATION

Above: Looking through the dining area to the west and Kapiti Island.

Left: Living area, under a lower ceiling, with the stairs to the viewing tower and the entrance to the right.

PARSONSONBEACHHOUSE

Above: Kitchen and dining area, with entry and stairs to tower at rear, and the garage beyond.

Right: The south-west corner of the house.

Facing page: On the deck, looking into the living area.

Right: Entry, showing corridor
to sleeping wing (at left), and
walkway leading to lawn and
garage on the east side.

Facing page, top left: Corridor
to the sleeping wing.

Facing page, top right: Stairs
to the tower.

Facing page, lower:
The garage is tucked behind
the bushes on the east
(street) side.

23 COX'S

STEVENS LAWSON
ARCHITECTS

WESTMERE,
AUCKLAND

2006

Previous spread: View up the
hall to front door.

Below: The house from the
spa and swimming pool on the
seaward side.

ARCHITECTS LOVE METAPHORS.
Lay readers of architects' design statements
or, especially, architects' award citations,
might think the profession has gone troppo
over tropes. Why so much figurative speech? In part,
metaphoric usage is a habit, but it's also a sign of good
intentions. Architects talk and write this way because
they are trying to communicate ideas that, if expressed
in the profession's own dialect — the language of site
and plan, programme and composition — would be
generally incomprehensible. Believe it or not, when
architects engage in linguistic transference, they're just
trying to connect.

Architecture being, among many things, a feed-
lot for already healthy egos, it's not surprising that its
practitioners prefer metaphors of epic connotation.
One of the all-time favourites is that of the journey.
The design of a house, the building of a house,
the act of moving through a house — they're all 'a
journey'. (Of course, as houses get bigger the term
risks reverting to mere description: some modern piles
should come with maps, not plans.) Sure enough,
Nicholas Stevens and Gary Lawson, the architects of
this house on a cliff above the Waitemata Harbour at
Westmere, and their clients, turn quickly to the J-word
when discussing the house, both as idea and realised
form. But, in this case, the reach doesn't seem at all
like a stretch. The house really is quite a trip.

The new house replaced a stucco bungalow that,
with its boat-builder owner, were survivors of the
old Westmere order. Before recent gentrification,
Westmere was an ordinary suburb that became

posher, but not much flasher, at its coastal edge. The
pronounced tidal behaviour of the Waitemata around
Cox's Bay repelled wealth, mud and money not being
natural neighbours. Well, not then; now all coasts are
desirable, no matter what the ebb tide reveals. The old
bungalow, with its sheds, concrete yard — the previous
owner was a very hard landscaper — and still-extant
jetty and boat ramp, formed a rambling compound, the
sort of set-up reasonably common around Auckland
down through the twentieth century, when the city
had a loose ease that, to the rest of a buttoned-up
country, was sinfully close to profligacy.

It would be hard to find a more telling sign of a
suburb's changing fortunes than the supplanting of an
accretion of artlessly functional structures by one of
Stevens Lawson's highly crafted bespoke houses. High
on the shortlist of every affluent discerning client,
sure-fire awards winner, and mediagenic to boot, the
practice inevitably attracts some professional envy.
The architect's F-word — 'fashionable' — might even
be uttered (to which Stevens Lawson might reply
that if you're going to do couture, it might as well be
haute). But the practice partners are intent on pushing
themselves and, perhaps, their clients, and extending
their range. Recently, for example, the practice has won
competitions to design a civic precinct in Queenstown
and a complex for Auckland City Mission.

The clients for the Cox's Bay House seem,
from an architect's perspective, close to ideal. They
had the means, motive and opportunity to commit
architecture, and they had ideas, but not closed minds.
In the brief for their new house, the clients set down

what they did and didn't want. For a start, they wanted a wooden house that was not 'a big Auckland box' and would resist easy periodisation; they didn't want too many right angles; they wanted 'secret things' rather than a 'what you see is what you get' open plan; they wanted courtyards; they didn't want a front fence or an assertive face to the street; they wanted calmness and serenity, and also 'a certain feeling of being on holiday'; and they wanted a house that was black, the colour of their previous home, a celebrated work of mid-century modernism, the Mann House (1960) in Mt Albert, designed by Ivan Juriss.

They've got what they asked for, and then some. This is a surprising house, or rather, a house of surprises. Unlike other new architect-designed houses in this street, which either pointedly reject the street or aggressively advance upon it, this house recedes from its public frontage. One could almost say it slithers or wriggles away from the street — the architects themselves call it a caterpillar — and this sense of shy withdrawal will only become more pronounced as the front planting grows. It takes confidence, on the part of clients and architect, to deal with a New Zealand suburban street in this manner. The dumb instrument of the fence is here replaced by a strategic approach, in which siting, form, colour and landscape are all deployed to safeguard the private realm. Defence in depth, it could be called. The critic Bill McKay, writing in *Architecture New Zealand* (March/April, 2006), described the house as 'stealth architecture'. Like the American bomber designed to keep a low radar profile, Stevens Lawson's house doesn't give much away.

As far as the public can see — from the street or out on the water — this is a house of two ends. What can't be appreciated from the outside is the nature and extent of the progress from point to point. Yes: the 'journey'. It's a long passage through this site — 60 metres from street to sea — and much of it is continuous. A terracotta path starts at the footpath, leads to the front entrance and just keeps going, right through the house, ramping down to follow the topography of the site. The orange brick road passes rooms pod-like in their privacy, and three interior courtyards, before it terminates at the kitchen, dining and living area, overlooking the lawn, the pool, and the Waitemata. By the time you get to this end of the house, you feel like you've come a long way; actually, you have come a long way, and you might think twice about going back. The doorbell response time might try the patience of the Jehovah's Witnesses.

The corridor is an extraordinary space, mainly because it has been given so much space. Stevens says it might be interpreted as an allusion to the hallway in a traditional villa, but it's less a hall, more a village street, taken indoors. It flows and winds, but is not smoothly sinuous. There is a certain jerky rhythm to Stevens Lawson's work, evidenced in this house by the juxtaposition of curved shapes and origami-like forms.

Self-admittedly, beauty is what the architects are after, but hardly conventional good looks. The practice seems wary of the bland competence that the computer can bring (anyone can do that!). Cue twists, turns, and clever contrivances: the journey as Odyssey.

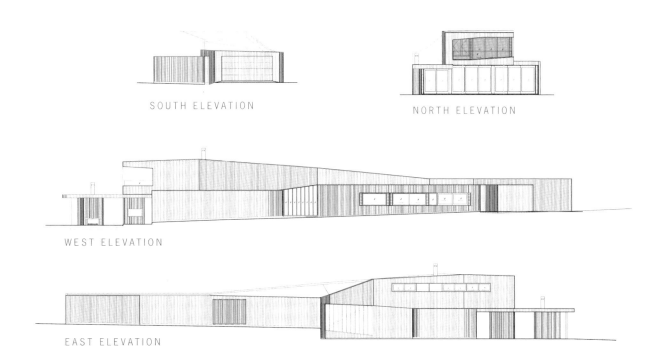

SOUTH ELEVATION

NORTH ELEVATION

WEST ELEVATION

EAST ELEVATION

View from the west, looking into the lower-level living areas and upper-level bedroom.

Right: Stairs from the hall up
to the main bedroom.

Facing page: Looking across
the dining table to the kitchen,
with a courtyard to the right.

1 living room
2 dining room
3 kitchen
4 store
5 lounge
6 entry
7 studio
8 garage
9 bedroom
10 ensuite
11 dressing
12 laundry
13 bathroom
14 terrace

FIRST FLOOR PLAN

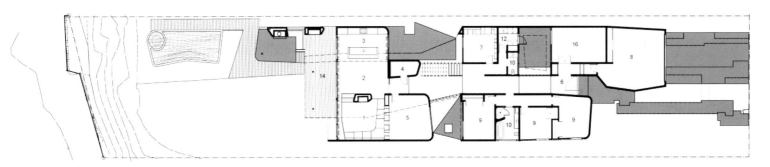

GROUND FLOOR PLAN

Facing page: Looking through the circular bathroom window into the main bedroom and out to sea.

Above: The bathroom, with shower on the right.

Left: Looking from the bedroom through the circular window to the bathroom.

Facing page: Looking from the courtyard on the east side through the kitchen to the sea.

Above: Looking from the kitchen at the back of the lounge fireplace.

Left: Street elevation.

Following spread, left: Looking from the bedroom deck west to the upper harbour.

Following spread, right: Sunset from the rear deck.

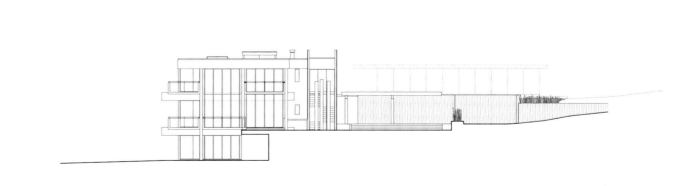

24 SARGENT–DUNN HOUSE

FAIRHEAD SANG &
CARNACHAN (1973)
FEARON HAY ARCHITECTS (2005)

REMUERA, AUCKLAND

REMUERA HAS LONG BEEN

the Auckland suburb where old money is most at home, and the new rich would like to be. It's a byword for established wealth, its national reputation earned through decades of Pavlonian responses in the polling booths. In election after election, no matter what carnage might be befalling the National Party around the country, Remuera could be counted on to remain True Blue. Not that the haute bourgeoisie was strident in its politics; it used to prefer its MPs to be professional types who would behave like gentlemen. Sitting serenely on the pillows of comfortable electoral majorities, they usually did. As for the constituents of the Hon. Member for Remuera, life in the streets on the suburb's northern slopes was about as stately as it got in New Zealand.

Imagine the surprise, then, when the Sargent House went up on one of those streets in the early 1970s. It even sounded like an upstart: what was a 'Sargent House' doing in an officer-class street? And as for its looks: the house, designed by Ron Sang, was a chunky concrete bruiser, with a flat top, jutting balconies and thrusting beams. It presented a slab of concrete, ribbed and mash-hammered, to anyone with the temerity to peep over the ficus-covered front wall. Concrete might have been OK for a Ministry of Works job — a government department, say, or the National Library, or even the Beehive — but surely it was out of place in a genteel neighbourhood of gabled and weather-boarded family homes? The Sargent House looked like a bit of Brit Brutalism; it was a

building that would have been quite at home on a new campus in Essex. To the neighbours the interloper must have must have been as palatable as a Pommy trade unionist to a National Party cabinet minister.

Concrete buildings often do not age gracefully, and Brutalist ones seldom do — like once-tough pugilists, they seem prematurely worse for wear, and usually stuck in their ways. (More extreme critics might say they were brain-damaged from the start.) Over time the Sargent House became rather fatigued, although it did receive some revivalist attention. It's quite conceivable that the house, although admired by architects who generally have a soft spot for tough styles and their profession's elder statesmen, might have been pulled down to make way for a completely new building. But while the Sargent House might not have wide appeal, it is the sort of building that does inspire particular affection. In 2002, the then-owners commissioned Fearon Hay to alter and enlarge the house, and adapt it to contemporary use. A thorough-going do-up, then, and if such a brief sometimes leads to a house's effective destruction, in this case it has ensured its salvation.

For a start, Fearon Hay have restored the house's relationship to its site. Actually, although the house is now twice the size — or rather, has twice the space, which is a different matter — it probably sits better on its 2000 square metre section than it ever did. The intention, says Jeff Fearon, was 'to get back to the idea of a building sitting in a park'. Clarity and coherence were the goals. Terracing along the north side has been extended and the pool reoriented to run, more companionably, across the face of the house

Previous spread: Looking across the pool to the new pavilion and carport which adjoin the existing building.

Facing page: Detail of the new carport and pavilion.

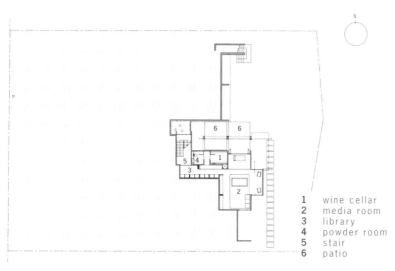

1 wine cellar
2 media room
3 library
4 powder room
5 stair
6 patio

BASEMENT PLAN

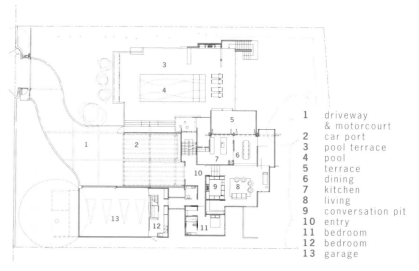

1 driveway & motorcourt
2 car port
3 pool terrace
4 pool
5 terrace
6 dining
7 kitchen
8 living
9 conversation pit
10 entry
11 bedroom
12 bedroom
13 garage

GROUND FLOOR PLAN

rather than head away from it. An over-abundance of steps and changes of level has been rationalised, and a clumsy ramp connecting house and terrace has been eliminated. The concrete carport/pergola to the west has been replaced by a simpler, less obviously supported form that, together with the adjacent new pavilion, lends horizontal balance to what was an overtly perpendicular building. On the lower east side, hedging has been removed, allowing for a long, uninterrupted stretch of lawn. The grounds, generally, have been rendered more formal, though the landscaping is not gimmicky and the planting is not fussy. The effect is to give a rather monumental house the space it deserves. In this setting, the house achieves a stillness and authority denied to similarly scaled houses stuffed onto disproportionately small sites. Forget Essex; the current owner is right — the grandeur of this house and the generosity of its site suggest a largesse that is positively North American.

Inside, the architects have pursued the same design course, tacking between subtraction and addition, restoration and reformation. Ron Sang's structure has been peeled back, repaired, and even occasionally moved; some spaces have been enclosed, some rooms have been inserted (very adroitly), and some formal elements have been added. But all the while, Fearon says, the original threshold has been observed. After a while in this house, you realise that much of the work that really mattered is work that cannot be seen. Structural rehabilitation wasn't just a necessity, it was an opportunity. So, for example, the scoring out of leaking joins for make-good injections into the concrete skin also enabled the builders to deal with a lot of chasing. Wherever possible, it seems, the messy business of a house's services — whether it be the drainage or the power supply — is handled with utmost discretion. The down pipes from the carport roof are encased in the concrete pillars; the wiring of the flat screen TV in the restored conversation pit is hidden in a stainless steel screen which itself disappears without trace into precisely cut holes in the bleached cedar ceiling. The appearance of another TV in freestanding guise, its leads and plugs visible, is a bit of a shock. (Supermarket shoppers used to vacuum-packed steak might be as surprised to see what's hanging in a butcher's back room.)

As crucial to the success of this project as the manipulations of interiors and the handling of details is the treatment of light — its admission and its framing. Sang framed the big windows of the Sargent House in bronze-coloured aluminium; Fearon Hay specified steel frames for those windows, and for the new windows and glazed doors they have added. The placement of the full-height windows, especially on the south side of the house, is very important — one window Fearon Hay put along the rear corridor leading to the new pavilion offers a nice, intimate prospect of a small courtyard, in counterpoint to the big north views — and the steel is a better match with the concrete. Aluminium seems a little arriviste; steel says you're here to stay. This house is one of the best reworkings of any New Zealand building in the last decade. It won its election in 2007: the New Zealand Institute of Architects gave it a supreme award.

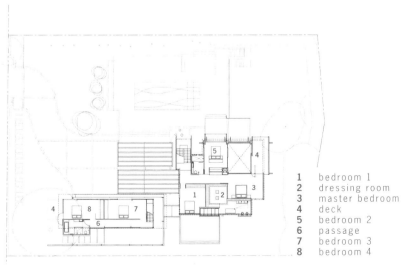

1 bedroom 1
2 dressing room
3 master bedroom
4 deck
5 bedroom 2
6 passage
7 bedroom 3
8 bedroom 4

FIRST FLOOR PLAN

Above: The north-east corner, showing the weighty, cantilevered forms of the original building.

Right: North elevation, showing the new double-height steel joinery outside the existing structure.

Looking from the new kitchen
into the double-height dining
room.

Looking from the dining room
back into the kitchen.

Above: Living area on the
main floor.

Facing page, top: Looking into
the reclaimed conversation pit
on the main floor.

Facing page, lower: The living
area from the conversation pit.

Above: Looking from the
garden to the new pavilion,
with bedrooms above and
garaging below.

Right: The view over the
carport through the chain-mail
exterior screens from the
upper-level bedrooms.

25 INNERHARBOURHOUSE

GEOFF RICHARDS
ARCHITECTS

DEVONPORT, AUCKLAND

1997, 2006

25

Previous spread and facing page: Looking though the house from the courtyard to the harbour and city beyond.

RAISED ABOVE A SEA wall, tucked against a cliff, coloured grey and looking hard, this house on genteel Stanley Point doesn't betray obvious domestic antecedents. Rather, it appears to be a super-evolved descendant of martial types: the concrete gun emplacements built to protect the approaches to a remote and nervous colony's major ports. A fine example of these little coastal forts survives on North Head, a couple of kilometres away. It's not just the house's location and materials, and its excellent lines of sight, that prompt such genealogical speculation; there's also the character of a near neighbour. The house is just along the bay from the base and dockyard where, on any given day, a good proportion of New Zealand's navy is at rest or under repair.

Devonport architect Geoff Richards has had two goes at this house. In the 1990s, for the original clients, he designed a house with a transparent upper level above a solid base — a glass top on a concrete bottom. This emphatically horizontal form echoed the striations of the cliff which the house was built on and against. From the street that runs along the spine of Stanley Point the house, behind its wall and gate, is practically invisible; its southern elevation is its public face, and that can only be seen from the harbour or the adjacent ferry wharf.

The house posed a dilemma common to coastal buildings oriented to take in south-facing views: how to maximise these views without minimising light, warmth and shelter? (Even on privileged Stanley Point, you can't always have it both ways.) The courtyard — not unusually, but in this case, cleverly — was the solution. On the north side of the house, Richards sited two protected terrace areas which admit light into the see-through upper level, and offer views across the harbour to Auckland's working port. The container wharves appear startlingly near; Stanley Point is where Auckland's harbour most closely approximates the intimacy of Sydney's. Going without a view of Auckland's inelegant harbour bridge is a small price to pay for such a prospect.

Richards returned to the house when its new owners wanted more of it. On the second time around, work included the conversion of the lower level from simple base structure to habitation — a job, the architect says, that was 'as much about tunnelling as construction'. (The lower level is something of a cave-with-a-view.) Staircases connecting the two levels were added at the eastern and western ends of the house; on the upper level, kitchen and dining areas have been extended. A visitor, moving through the house, might find the new work a seamless extension of the old — notwithstanding a discrete aluminium strip set into a wall to acknowledge the meeting of existing and new, slightly different concrete flooring — but Richards says that with the additions 'the whole composition of the south side had to change'. The increased complexity of the house can be read on the sea-side elevation where the introduction of vertical elements has produced a form that is less end-to-end and more up-and-down.

Rather than attempting to disguise or downplay the external evidence of the changes he had made to the house, Richards took the opportunity to 'add to its formal richness'. (A phrase a layperson might translate

UPPER LEVEL PLAN

1 entry
2 courtyard
3 pool
4 garage
5 bedroom
6 study
7 living
8 kitchen
9 dining
10 balcony

new areas shaded

as 'make more interesting'.) On the south side, ground-level rooms required windows; sections of the concrete panel wall have been taken up to balustrade height; there is a new two-storey glass element; rusted steel has been attached to a portion of blockwork. The balustrades are made of stainless steel mesh. A finer steel mesh flanks the interior staircases. There have been changes, as well, on the north side, where the roof to the west has been extended to give more continuity to the form and greater privacy against future development. (Architects must always anticipate neighbourly self-interest.)

On this site, total abstinence from nautical references would be perverse, but Richards has used maritime analogies in moderation. The steel balustrade mesh, he allows, alludes to the gates on the Auckland ferry wharf. There is a porthole in the wall of the downstairs bathroom and circular cut-outs in the roofs above the upper level courtyards, and the house inside and out is warship grey. But the relationship of house to site is a matter of connections, not gestures. Those connections — to water, harbour and land — are stronger now that the new staircases have made them overt.

Richards, who over the course of a 30-year career has seen Devonport change from a suburb of characters to a Character Suburb, has patiently and cannily navigated his way through the regulations that barnacle any development on a littoral strip designated both a coastal conservation and a heritage zone. Not for him or his clients, on this sea wall and against this cliff, a lightweight response from the driftwood school.

Instead, Richards has produced a house that is at once deep and transparent. And reassuringly solid: if New Zealand's strategic situation were suddenly to worsen, surely a salvaged cannon could be slid across that polished concrete floor.

The city at night provides a dramatic backdrop.

LOWER LEVEL PLAN

1 bedroom
2 music
3 home theatre

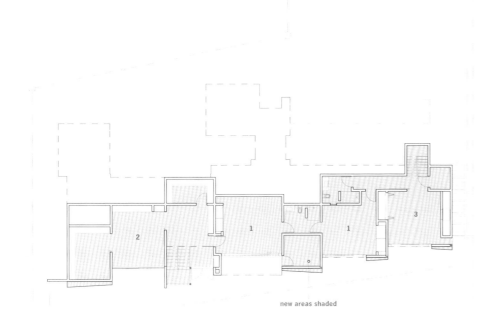

new areas shaded

Above: On the seaward
terrace, looking to the stairs
descending from the study.

Right: Stairwell on the seaward
side, showing reflections of
the port across the harbour.

Facing page: Pool and
courtyard.

Above and top right: In the
corridor leading to the upstairs
bedroom wing.

Right: Detail of the kitchen.

Top of the stairs outside the main-floor study.

Living room, with the courtyard and pool to the left, and Devonport's naval dockyard in the background.

Looking across the pool and
courtyard into the house and
towards the city.

LINDALE BACH
40

HERBST ARCHITECTS

Lance and Nicola Herbst established their Auckland-based practice in 2001. Herbst Architects has won five New Zealand Institute of Architects (NZIA) local awards and one NZIA New Zealand award, five of the six awards being for baches and beach houses.

Design team: Lance and Nicola Herbst
Contractor: Paragon Construction
Interior design: Herbst Architects
Landscape design: Herbst Architects
Landscape installation: John Sutton

HUGHES–KINUGAWA
HOUSE 190

ANDREW LISTER ARCHITECT

Auckland-based Andrew Lister Architect was formed by principal Andrew Lister in 1999. The practice works on both residential and commercial projects and is the recipient of many national and local awards. The Hughes–Kinugawa house won a NZIA New Zealand award in 2003.

Design team: Andrew Lister
Builder: Laurie McMurtrie Builders
Structural engineer: Law Sue Consulting
Landscaping: Client

PARSONSON BEACH
HOUSE 264

PARSONSON ARCHITECTS

Wellington-based Parsonson Architects was formed by Gerald Parsonson in 1987. Its current projects include apartment buildings, retail work and housing. The practice has won numerous awards, including NZIA Supreme and New Zealand awards and the *Home & Entertaining* Home of the Year award in 2001.

Design team: Gerald Parsonson, Andreas Cherry
Contractor: Sutton Builders
Interior designer: Gerald and Kate Parsonson
Landscape designer: Gerald and Kate Parsonson

WAKATIPU BASIN
HOUSE 52

BUTLER HOUSE
164

SARGENT–DUNN
HOUSE 290

FEARON HAY ARCHITECTS

Established in 1998, this Auckland-based practice is a partnership between principals Jeff Fearon and Tim Hay. A multi-award winner, among the practice's most prestigious honours are a NZIA Supreme award in 2007 for the Sargent-Dunn House and the *Home & Entertaining* Home of the Year award in 2000. In 2003 *Wallpaper** magazine (UK) placed Fearon Hay in its top 25 emerging architects list.

Sargent–Dunn House
Design team: Jeff Fearon, Tim Hay
Contractor: Graydon Construction

Wakatipu Basin House
Design team: Jeff Fearon, Tim Hay
Engineeer: Holmes Consultants (Queenstown)
Contractor: D&M Builders (foreman Mark Dickson)

Butler House
Design team: Jeff Fearon, Tim Hay
Contractor: Jon Armstrong Builders

ARAPAI–URALE
HOUSE 30

VERNON RETREAT
66

MALCOLM WALKER ARCHITECTS

A sole partnership since 1985, Auckland-based Malcolm Walker Architects does one-off housing, alterations and small commercial works. The practice has won 11 NZIA awards, including two New Zealand awards.

Vernon Retreat
Design team: Malcolm Walker
Builder: Gordon Jowsey
Interiors: Penny Vernon

Arapai–Urale House
Design team: Malcolm Walker, Jeremy Smith
Builders: M F Astley Ltd (foreman, Rob Bremner)
Interiors: Penny Vernon

CROSSON CLARKE CARNACHAN

HALL HOUSE
198

Auckland-based Crosson Clarke Carnachan Architects designs coastal and rural homes, farm park developments, and large-scale residential, commercial, institutional and healthcare projects. Established by Ken Crosson, Paul Clarke and Simon Carnachan in 2004, the practice has won numerous awards, including a NZIA Supreme award in 2004 and the *Home & Entertaining* Home of the Year award in 2003, both for the Coromandel Bach.

CARNACHAN HOUSE
232

Hall House
Design team: Paul Clarke
Engineer: Smith & Henry
Contractor: Breen Construction
Landscape architect: Wraight & Associates

Carnachan House

COROMANDEL BACH
242

Design team: Simon Carnachan, Corbett Madden
Engineer: Structure Design
Contractor: P W & J A Hari
Interior designer: Robyn Carnachan
Landscape architect: Suzanne Turley Design

Coromandel Bach
Design team: Ken Crosson
Engineer: Thorne Dwyer Structures

DAVE LAUNDER ARCHITECT

Kapiti Coast-based Dave Launder Architects was established in 1972. In 2005 it was a finalist in the Year of the Built Environment award. The Kaitawa House won a NZIA Supreme award in 2007.

KAITAWA HOUSE
128

Design team: Dave Launder
Landscape designer/ecologist: Isobel Gabites

STEVENS LAWSON ARCHITECTS

ONETANGI BEACH
HOUSE 152

Stevens Lawson Architects was established in Auckland in 2002 by Nicholas Stevens and Gary Lawson. The practice works on residential, public, cultural, interior, urban and landscape projects. Stevens Lawson has won numerous awards for domestic architecture, including a NZIA Supreme award. The Cox's Bay House won the *Home & Entertaining* Home of the Year award in 2007.

COX'S BAY HOUSE
274

Onetangi Beach House
Design team: Nicholas Stevens, Gary Lawson and Philip Graham
Engineer: Markplan Consulting
Contractor: Tomik Ltd
Landscaper: O² Landscapes

Cox's Bay House
Design team: Nicholas Stevens, Gary Lawson and Philip Graham
Engineer: Markplan Consulting
Contractor: Graham Mauger Builders
Landscaper: Patrick Stokes

GODWARD GUTHRIE ARCHITECTURE

CROSS HOUSE
208

Matthew Godward and Julian Guthrie established Godward Guthrie in 1999. The Auckland-based practice focuses on residential, retail and commercial architecture and has won several NZIA local awards including one for the Cross House (2006).

Design team: Julian Guthrie, Philip Jarvis
Engineer: Brown and Thomson
Contractor: Latham Construction
Interior designer: Architect
Landscape architect: Price and Humphries

RIVERSIDE ROAD
HOUSE 16

ORIENTAL BAY
HOUSE 78

ARCHITECTURE WORKSHOP

Wellington-based Architecture Workshop (AW) was established by Chris Kelly on his return from Europe in 1992. In 2003 AW won an ar+d emerging architecture award in the United Kingdom for the Peregine winery in Central Otago. AW won a NZIA Supreme award in 2004 for the winery and in 2005 for its work on the enhancement of Oriental Bay, Wellington.

Riverside Road House

Design team: Chris Kelly, James Fenton, Melissa Green, Arindam Sen, Stephen Waterman
Structural engineer: Dunning Thornton
Consultants: Alistair Cattenach
Contractor: Ron Allen
Landscape architect: Megan Wraight

Oriental Bay House

Design team: Chris Kelly, James Fenton, Melissa Green, Arindam Sen, Stephen Waterman
Structural engineer: Dunning Thornton
Consultants: Alistair Cattenach
Contractor: Ron Allen

McCAHON HOUSE
102

PAROA BAY HOUSE
178

PETE BOSSLEY ARCHITECTS

Pete Bossley Architects was established in Auckland in 1997. During his time as a director at Jasmax Architects Bossley was the design principal jointly in charge of the design and documentation of the Museum of New Zealand Te Papa Tongarewa. Bossley is the recipient of many awards including, most recently, a NZIA Supreme award in 2006 for the Paroa Bay House.

McCahon House

Design team: Pete Bossley, Andrea Bell, Tim Lane, Don McKenzie, Karen Ngan Kee
Structural engineer: Brown and Thomson
Contractor: PSL (Phil and Steve Leach)
Interior designer: Penny Vernon

Paroa Bay House

Design team: Pete Bossley, James Downey, Mike Jackson, Paul Somerford, Andrea Bell, Tim Lane, Don McKenzie, Karen Ngan Kee
Structural engineer: Brown and Thomson
Interior designer: Pete Bossley Architects, Timi Pinfold
Project manager: Peter Healey
Contractor: David and Brian Mather
Landscape designer: Gary Boyle

WALKER HOUSE
254

MITCHELL AND STOUT ARCHITECTS

David Mitchell and Julie Stout formed Mitchell and Stout Architects in Auckland in 1990. The partnership has won many awards, among the most recent being a NZIA New Zealand award in 2005 for the Unitec Landscape and Plant Sciences Staff Studies Building and the *Home & Entertaining* Home of the Year award in 2005. Also in 2005, David Mitchell received the NZIA Gold Medal, his profession's highest honour.

Design team: David Mitchell, Julie Stout, Jeremy Purcell
Engineer: Dave Shilton and Associates
Contractor: Rod Percival Builders
Interior consultant: Jen Pack

HUDSON-YOUNG
HOUSE 90

COOK SARGISSON TARRANT AND PIRIE

This Auckland-based practice was formed in 1968, originally as a design-focused residential practice. It has subsequently grown into a mid-sized practice involved in most areas of architecture, urban design, master planning and interior design. The directors are Marshall Cook, Peter Sargisson, Simon Pirie and Guy Tarrant. The practice has won five NZIA New Zealand awards, and numerous NZIA local awards.

Design team: Guy Tarrant, Graham Wrack, Tim Fairweather
Structural engineer: John Allen
Main contractor: Bradshaw and Loane

NORTH SHORE
HOUSE 116

ARCHITECTUS

Formed 20 years ago by Patrick Clifford, Malcolm Bowes and Michael Thomson, Architectus works across residential, commercial and public buildings, urban design, planning and interiors. It has recently united with a group of Australian architects to form offices in Auckland, Sydney, Melbourne, Brisbane and Shanghai. It is a winner of numerous NZIA awards at all levels, with the North Shore House winning a NZIA Supreme award in 2004.

Design team: Patrick Clifford, Malcolm Bowes, Michael Tompson, Carsten Auer, James Mooney, Prue Fea, Stephen Bird, Lance Adolph, Sean Kirton, John Lambert, Juliet Pope, Rachael Rush, Raymond Soh
Structural engineer: Thorne Dwyer Structures
Contractor: Good Brothers
Landscape architect: Rod Barnett

INNER HARBOUR
HOUSE 302

GEOFF RICHARDS ARCHITECTS

Geoff Richards is the principal of this eponymous, Auckland-based practice, which he established in 1973. The practice is the recipient of numerous NZIA awards, the most recent being a NZIA New Zealand award in 2005 for the Seacliffe House, Auckland, and in 2006 for the Inner Harbour House. In 2005 Geoff Richards was awarded the NZIA President's Award for services to architecture.

Design team: Geoff Richards, Ray van Wayenburg, Annette Alexander
Engineer: Airey Consultants
Contractor: Bonham Builders

ZINC HOUSE
138

PATTERSON ASSOCIATES

Established in Auckland in 1990, Patterson Associates is engaged in residential, apartment and commercial work, under the direction of Andrew Patterson. The practice is the recipient of many awards, including, most recently, a NZIA New Zealand award in 2002 for Site 3, a NZIA Supreme award in 2003 for Cumulus and a NZIA New Zealand award in 2006 for Stratis.

Design team: Andrew Patterson, Trevor Allen
Engineer: Holmes Consulting
Contractor: Rod Percival Builders

VAN ASCH HOUSE
220

FELICITY WALLACE ARCHITECTS

Former design tutor Felicity Wallace's practice, now based in Marton, was established in 1989 and specialises in residential work. The van Asch house in Queenstown won a NZIA New Zealand award in 2005.

Design team: Felicity Wallace, Paul Spooner, Anna Tong, James Young, Kim Phillip
Structural engineer: Tyndall and Hanham
Electrical engineer: Electrical Consulting Services
Main contractor: Amalgamated Builders, Queenstown (foreman, Roger Kennedy)

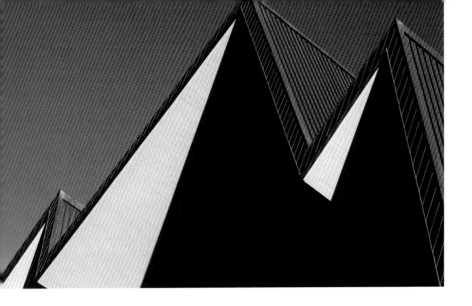

THIS IS NOT A BUILDING

. . . this is a photograph of a building. Photography may appear to reflect the world but really it makes a new one: its core action is not one of recording, but of transforming. And as critic and curator Christina Barton writes, 'the distance photography inserts between object and image is a necessary condition of the medium.' In other words, it can't help it. Yet it is for its veracity that it is valued. Indeed it is a function of the essential nature of photography that the photograph is mistaken for its subject. The viewers feel they are seeing the thing, feel they can see past or through the photograph to the thing in itself. In fact there is a tendency to forget about the messenger altogether. This is what Roland Barthes means when he writes 'the photograph is always invisible, it's not it that we see'. And fair enough too. This book, for example, has appeal as a book of houses, not photographs, but in truth it is somewhere in between.

Curiously, the plainer the photographic approach, the greater its apparent objectivity, the more misleading it may be. We can all dismiss an image constructed with theatrical pyrotechnics, exaggerated distortions or heavy-handed post-production as a deceit. But we are all more persuaded by a subtle approach.

And a plain or apparently objective photographic style is the stock-in-trade of the architectural photographer. There is a lot of this approach in this book. I love it, not because it is truer or more neutral but because it can make a striking image. Architectural photographers risk becoming over-obsessed with straight verticals, and the attempt to reproduce the elevations of a building as they were drawn is usually a starting point of any shoot.

This approach gives the building a singularity, an heroic, almost startling, quality that it may or may not be able to live up to. But then, the camera with its relentless, staring, one-point perspective can be a bit of a bully. Like a dogged council inspector, the camera has an unerring tendency to highlight a subcontractor's unfortunate handiwork or an architect's infelicitous detailing that would not be all that obvious in the flesh.

The camera, then, is fairly poor at translating spatial volume to its two dimensions, not much good at describing a building's programme, and no use at all at giving the temperature, smell, sound, or feel of being there. In truth, photography is a beguiling but deceptive road to architecture. And I love it. Brilliant at surface and mood, it invents its own theatre from the everyday, gives form and order to a messy world. It dissembles marvellously, an unreliable witness to concrete fact and human experience. But, for better or for worse, for feeding our dreams and longings it is perfect. Perfect because of its limitations. It idealises, it sings up. It provides a sufficiently reduced but convincing version of life to give a perfect toe-hold for our desires.

In 1938 the English architect Goodhart-Rendell warned, 'the modern architectural drawing is interesting, the photograph magnificent, the building an unfortunate but necessary stage between the two.' And yet, and yet, for me there is something wonderful in facing that same set of problems: half-showing/half-hiding the object in front of me, struggling to make hard matter sing, wrestling with the medium to make something interesting, something beautiful, perhaps even truthful, go on in that little place in the dark.

Patrick Reynolds, 2007

TECHNICAL NOTE

I always am really interested when practitioners discuss the practicalities of their craft. And with photography on some level the apparatus is the thing, perhaps even more interesting in this period of such significant technological change. So, the gear. Almost all the projects in this book were shot with Canon digital cameras, the breakthrough 1Ds and a 1Ds Mark 2. The exceptions (Carnachan House, Mace House and Otama House) were shot on Fujichrome with V series Hasselblads. Prepress was by Sjoerd Langeveld at Labtec.